Worship Musician!

Presents

THE WORSHIP DRUM BOOK

THE WORSHIP DRUM BOOK

Concepts to Empower Excellence

Carl Albrecht

Hal Leonard Books
An Imprint of Hal Leonard Corporation

Published in 2013 by Hal Leonard Books
An Imprint of Hal Leonard Corporation
7777 West Bluemound Road
Milwaukee, WI 53213

Trade Book Division Editorial Offices
33 Plymouth St., Montclair, NJ 07042

PHOTO CREDITS
Figures 2.1, 9.1, 9.2 by Frank DeJong; Figures 2.2, 3.1, 3.3 by CMS Productions; Figure 3.2 by Paul Arellano; Figure 8.4 by Mike Overlin; Figures 4.1, 4.2, 4.3, 4.4, 4.5, 5.1, 6.1, 7.1, 7.2, 8.1, 8.2, 8.3, 8.5, 14.1, 14.2, 14.3 by Carl Albrecht

All music score examples and chart sketches by Carl Albrecht
The song "You Are the One" by Carl and Leann Albrecht

Printed in the United States of America

Book design by Mayapriya Long, Bookwrights
Book composition by Kristina Rolander

Library of Congress Cataloging-in-Publication Data
Albrecht, Carl (Drummer)
The worship drum book : concepts to empower excellence / Carl Albrecht.
pages cm
Includes bibliographical references and index.
1. Drum--Instruction and study. 2. Drum set--Instruction and study. 3. Contemporary Christian music--Instruction and study. I. Title.
MT662.A53 2013
786.9'1930882--dc23
2012046906

ISBN 9781476814155

www.halleonardbooks.com

For my wife Leann,
who journeys with me on this amazing life adventure,
and the Lord, Jesus Christ, who ordains and guides our every step.
We live for the glory of His name.

Contents

Preface

The Worship Drum Book is a drummer's guide for playing drums, both in contemporary churches and in traditional churches transitioning into using full rhythm sections rather than just organ or piano. Concepts for touring with ministry groups and worship artists are also covered. But more than just being a drum method book, this writing dives deeply into the spiritual dynamics of being a musician for the Lord.

With over 30 years of experience in the modern worship movement, I've learned a lot about what drummers need to know to adapt to modern music being brought into the church. Bringing drum kits into the church, especially older traditional sanctuaries, has sometimes been a very controversial issue, so drummers have to be sensitive to this and yet play with authority and confidence.

This book not only addresses some traditional drumming techniques and concepts, but it also explains the unique role a drummer/musician has as a minstrel in the house of the Lord. Developing great drumming skills along with an understanding of spiritual matters is of the utmost importance. Welcome to this different kind of drum tutorial.

Acknowledgments

What makes a musician an artist? What is the spark that becomes a flame? Years of listening and learning are a lifelong process that began early. The first inspirations of music that caused me to move to a drumbeat, tap out a rhythm, hum a tune, and learn the poetry of songs surrounded me. I was planted in good ground.

Growing up in a musical family, I guess I could not escape the magnet of music. My father played guitar, sang, and was a bandleader his whole life, like his father before him. My mother grew up playing piano and organ in church, and played in my grandfather's band, where she met Dad. Although they never forced their children to play or study music, it seemed a natural progression that my older sister, Cathy; my younger brother, Doug; and myself all found the love of music early on. Each of us gravitated to the sounds we loved. Guitars, bass, piano, and vocal performances poured out of our home in St. Charles, Missouri. I became the drummer. I'm eternally grateful to my parents and siblings for those early inspirations.

I was also fortunate to have instruction from extremely talented and inspiring people. Fred Pierce, Kevin Gianino, and Kevin Sims were my early drum-kit teachers. During my Webster University days, I added classical percussion studies with John Kasica of the St. Louis Symphony while continuing drum-set lessons with Kevin Sims.

Piano was also part of my weekly training. Linda Eberhardt grounded me in music theory and a variety of piano styles that always kept me on my toes. That solid foundation of musical training led me to continue piano studies throughout my college years, even though my focus was on drums and percussion. A huge thank-you goes out to these teachers and all of those I've gleaned from as a growing musician. And I'm still learning now. Even though I teach quite a bit in master classes, clinics, and the occasional private lesson, I still love to learn.

I absolutely believe in God giving talents and gifts to mankind. All of these chapters in my life are no accident. The artistic spark, the genetic connection, the mentors, and all of the inspiration give evidence to God's blueprint in action. While all of these musical juices were flowing, I was always involved in a strong faith community. And I found that even more inspiring than the music itself.

A real love for the Lord and all things related to Him were in my heart from a very early age. I was blessed to be around real people with real faith. Looking back, I even see this as part of the plan the Lord designed for me. I always wanted to know Him more and honor the Lord with my life. I even thought of becoming a priest at one time. But the music was always there, and I felt like there was a calling in that as well.

In those intense college days, it wasn't wild living that tested me but the strain of pursuing my musical studies, classwork, and playing in bands. Burnout was hitting hard! Nothing felt right in my life at that time. As I sought the Lord for direction during that season, it became clear that I was really focused on what I wanted and had not given myself to God being in control of my life. I believed in God, but He was not Lord. And there is a difference. In the book of James, chapter 2, verse 5, it says that even the demons believe in God and tremble with fear. They don't follow Him; they just know He's there. This revelation hit me like a ton of bricks at a significant time in my life. So I started fresh with my faith. In that season, I renewed my faith on God's terms. I asked Jesus into my heart and dedicated my life to Him. I declared Him, Jesus, as Lord—not Carl. This started a whole new journey in my life.

All of my studying, working, and decisions were placed in the Lord's hands. How He wanted me to navigate life was His call. My goal was now to live according to what I felt was the Lord's will in my life. And He was definitely directing my steps.

I finished college with a degree in music and lots of playing experience already under my belt. But the doors that were opening led me to play and record with many Christian artists and play drums in ministry situations. Without any effort or planning, my musical work was being guided into the modern praise and worship movement that was, at that time, just gaining momentum. And so the hand of God was writing my story, and I was making my best effort to live it out with as much soul searching as possible. I've always lived wanting to do things right.

So with all sincerity, I thank the Lord for what He's done in my life, and for all of the people He used to guide my journey into His purposes for me. From my family and friends that encouraged me, to my teachers and mentors that trained me and challenged me to be better than I was at any one moment in time. There is always more.

Beyond words, I'm blessed with an amazing life partner who continues the journey with me. My wife, sweet Leann, I'm honored you chose to walk this wonderful, crazy life with me. God has knitted us together very well indeed. I love you more than I really have words to say. And I am humbled and so grateful for your encouragement, inspiration, and constant help in the journey the Lord has placed before both of us. Step by step we follow Him together.

And so, I dedicate this book to Jesus and His wonderful kingdom work in my life. I am His minstrel. Join me in the journey. If you have invited Jesus into your life, He will never leave you or forsake you. He is the way, the truth, and the life! And what a great, wonderful life in Him it is!

Introduction

I know this is going to be a very different kind of drum instruction book for many of you. We usually expect pages of drumsticking exercises, groove patterns, new coordination studies, and much more—all designed to launch us into the next level of our playing. There will be some of that, and I do love to be challenged in my chops building too. But the real goal of this book is to help you understand your calling as a minstrel for the Lord in the modern worship world.

I've played for many years, and there's always more to learn. That growing and learning should never stop for any musician. There is a mountain of educational material on the mechanics of playing, and we should all keep on climbing. It is exciting to grow in our skill, but there's more.

The focus of this book is to go beyond the talent and chops building—maybe I should say to add to it or empower your skill. That's what I want as I grow in my drum vocabulary: not just to play the notes, but to have the drums speak what's in my heart. The minstrels of the Lord are here on the Earth to declare the praises and the greatness of the true living God! I hope to share in these pages how the drummer in ministry situations becomes a vital partner to worship leaders and ministers. Yes, we'll learn how to grow in the skill the Lord has given each of us. But more importantly, I pray you catch the vision for why God gave you the passion to pour yourself into such a powerful instrument as the drums.

Welcome to the journey of discovering the spirit behind the artistry of the modern worship drummer.

THE WORSHIP DRUM BOOK

1

A Drummer in the House of the Lord

It's a great privilege to play music for the Lord and to help people experience the presence of God through this music. I believe musicians and singers are the gatekeepers to His presence for the church and the whole Earth. All believers have a call to be worshippers, but the artists have a significant role in being the leaders. We are not better people or God's favorites. We were just made for this purpose: to create a space where we can all meet with the Lord. That's our job, our calling.

> *You have made them to be a kingdom and priests to serve our God.*
>
> —Revelation 5:10

> *The Levites—all who were skilled in playing musical instruments—had charge of the laborers and supervised all the workers from job to job.*
>
> —II Chronicles 34: 12–13

Being a musician is such a joy. In any playing situation, I feel a sense of calling or destiny in what I do. But I am often asked what it is I feel in particular during a worship event or church service. What is going on that stirs such joy and celebration, or sometimes intercession and supplication? So I will dig deep to see if I can explain the experience that seems so beyond words. Help me, Lord!

The Training of a Modern Minstrel

The training for church musicians should be twofold. Both technical and spiritual disciplines are a must.

all of them trained and skilled in music for the Lord

—I Chronicles 25:7

So besides the hours of practice and study it takes to hone our musical skills, we also need to pursue spiritual disciplines. I know for a musician this can seem like a big responsibility. You may be thinking, "Hey, Carl, I just want to play drums in the band. Give me a break!" But stay with me here, and I believe you'll find something in your playing that perhaps you've never experienced before. It's so important to understand this spiritual dynamic to being a musician before covering any technical ideas.

My technical training involves practicing new ideas. I buy new drum books, videos, and CDs. I go to all the drum and percussion clinics I can fit into my schedule. Cruising the web for new drum ideas is an amazing resource too. Just type a concept in a search box, and there are hundreds of links that pop up. I've also started looking for a new teacher. That's right! After 30 years of playing professionally, I'm looking for someone to help me get to the next level. I like working on new grooves and new songs, and just having fun learning more about the gift the Lord has placed in me. We will discuss many of these ideas throughout this book.

The spiritual studying is just as important. I've just finished reading Don Potter's book *Facing the Wall* and *God Songs* by Paul Baloche and Jimmy and Carol Owens. One book is more about the heart issues of being a worshipper. It's a story of Don's personal journey of learning to walk with the Lord and listen to His voice, not just as a musician, but also as a dedicated follower of Christ. The other book discusses songwriting concepts. Paul, Jimmy, and Carol go in depth into songwriting techniques that have been part of their creative process for years. Yes, there is a spiritual dynamic to it, but they really focus on the discipline and tools of the art of songwriting. Both books and others I read stir something deep in my spirit about the calling God has on my life as a worship drummer/musician/priest in the house of the Lord. I continue to look for material that helps me grow in my spiritual and musical gifts, including Bible study. Here's a list of some great devotional writings I recommend to every musician.

1. *The Pursuit of God* by A.W. Tozer
2. *Facing the Wall* by Don Potter
3. *The Practice of the Presence of God* by Brother Lawrence
4. *Warrior Poets of the Twenty-First Century* by Robin Mark
5. *A Heart to Drum* by Terl Bryant

You have also been called if you are playing for any worship event. There are no accidents in the kingdom of God. The Lord has given you an assignment. Even if music is not your career, you have got to grab hold of the importance of being a worship musician. Don't fall into the trap of not caring or trying because this work is not bringing in a paycheck.

Having a Spiritual Community

It's also critical to stay involved in a local church or fellowship group. Don't just hide out at home reading the Bible. Being personally disciplined is good, but stay connected to the body of Christ at large. And I don't necessarily mean church, as we know it. It could be just a group of people in your life that have the same desire to grow in their faith. This could be a regular prayer meeting, a Bible study, or some other fellowship setting. There are things we only learn while in relationship to other believers. The sense of community and covering are vital in surviving the journey of life.

My wife, Leann, and I love being in worship services with our church family, hearing the Word of God preached and rejoicing when the testimonies of God's faithfulness are shared. Is the church perfect? No. And neither are we. It's just important to find a place where the Lord plants you and flourish there. Build relationships with God's people. Sometimes my artsy friends say I'm the church guy. They'll say I really promote being in a local church or community of believers. I think that's because artists or creative types tend to be loners. But I've seen too many talented people flounder because they had no spiritual family or community to help them. I know this whole idea could lead to a very lengthy debate, but let's just say don't be a lone ranger. No man or woman is an island.

> *Let us not give up meeting together, as some are in the habit of doing, but let us encourage one another.*
>
> —Hebrews 10:25

A Spiritual Life

The spiritual life of a musician affects how he or she worships. If you are just playing the instrument or doing the gig, and not pressing into the presence of God when you play, then you are only doing half of the job. I personally believe if you are not pursuing the Lord like the worship leader or *lead worshipper*, you could be dead weight in a worship band. I know that's strong talk, but I've seen it happen. Musicians and singers who don't join worship leaders in the pursuit of God seem to weigh them down or wear them out. This means having a prayer life, spending time in the Word, and when playing, turning your heart toward the Lord.

When you are fully engaging your heart and soul into the worship experience, something happens. What this really means is giving your full attention to the Lord and to the music when you are worshipping. Not only should we love the Lord with all our heart, mind, soul, and strength, but we should also play our instruments with that same intensity. Worship leaders have said to me, "Carl, it feels like you're pushing or compelling me to go after God deeper when you're playing. What is that?" I'm not totally sure what that all encompasses. All I know is that I'm as desperate for the presence of God as they are. I'm hungry for the Lord and want to honor and bless Him with the music we are playing. And I want to draw the congregation into that same attitude of heart. It could have something to do with the fact that the Lord shows up in a special way when we play together as a unit. When the whole band plays with as much skill as they can and with the same passion, the Lord responds to the heart cry of His people.

> *when they made a sound as one ... the glory of the Lord had filled the house of God.*
>
> —II Chronicles 5:13-14

Preparing to Worship

Before worship starts, I'm praying. I talk to the Lord about what He would like to see happen during the worship. Even as I prepare my drums and music, I have my *spiritual antenna* up, trying to sense what's going on in the atmosphere. Sometimes the Lord convicts me of something, and I have to repent. There are times I feel intercession rise up in me because there is a battle raging in the spirit realm. So I will focus my prayers on that target until I feel the burden for it is lifted.

I'm also paying attention to the lead worshipper. How does he feel today? What does he want to accomplish in the worship time? Also, how is the rest of the team doing? I try to sense what the spiritual climate is in the rest of the band. Everyone is important! Becoming a band that is unified is more than just getting the music right. It is just as important to be one in spirit and purpose. So you see, there is a lot happening before the music even begins.

Let the Worship Begin

When the music starts and we're getting into the flow of worship, I have a sense of being on guard. Yes, I'm doing the job of a musician too. I always want the music to be played with as much excellence as I am capable of. I'm checking the song list, checking my equipment, setting click tracks, and listening to the other musicians, but there is so much more. Don't miss your primary spiritual purpose while also attending to the mechanics of music.

As the worship continues, I listen to any stories being shared or prayers that come forth. Maybe the worship leader pauses because he senses something from the Lord. I go there with him in my heart. I start to pray for him and pray with him. It's never just about playing the drums. I'm asking the Lord to help us meet Him where He is and do as He pleases. If a pastor comes up to pray or read, I stay engaged. I listen and watch carefully for anything that is stirring in the spiritual atmosphere of the meeting. What are the leaders and the other team members doing? Is something stirring in the congregation? Stay alert! Never lose focus on the most important part of being a worship drummer. Be a worshipper!

Musically, I have no idea what I will do next if we're moving beyond the song list. Yes, I do know what to do when playing the song arrangements, but in worship there is always more than that. There are the spontaneous musical moments that coordinate with what happens spiritually in worship. As I'm playing, all of a sudden sounds will rise up out of me, like the groaning of the spirit in prayer. A loud cymbal crash, a thundering tom fill, or maybe a light tap of a cymbal or triangle, or who knows, maybe I'll just keep a steady pulsing groove moving along. It's like I'm playing the lyrics of a song or the words of a prayer, or just underscoring what's happening at the moment. The actual notes or technique of playing is no longer a concern. Yes, I'm "in tune" and unified with the team. I am also reaching out to the Lord and praying for His purposes to be fulfilled.

In all of these instances, I'm aware of being in the presence of God and wanting the people to feel free to enter in with us. I'm standing guard at the gates of the presence of God so the lead worshipper (worship leader) can take the people into this most powerful experience. That sounds pretty wild, doesn't it? Well, that's what it feels like to me. Yet, my words seem so incapable of creating a complete picture. I just pray it helps you discover why the Lord made you a musician. I believe that is to minister to Him with the talent and gifts He's given you, and to help people experience the Lord when you play and worship Him.

> *they will be coming down from a high place with lyres, tambourines, flutes and harps … and they will be prophesying. The Spirit of the Lord will come upon you in power, and you will prophesy with them; and you will be changed into a different person.*
>
> —I Samuel 10:5–11

> *David would take his harp and play. Then relief would come to Saul; he would feel better, and the evil spirit would leave him.*
>
> —I Samuel 16:23

Pursue and stir up the gift within you as a priest in the house of the Lord, and you will see the Lord honor your efforts. Of course we don't force God to do anything, but I know that He desires to see us fulfill the calling He has given us. The Lord truly inhabits the praises of His people. And He said He will be found when we search for Him with all of our heart. Even though I feel I know Him well, I'm still searching—still reaching. "Lord, I'm desperate for You!" Blessings to you as you also reach out to Him.

2

Worship Drumming Essentials

I've been fortunate to play drums and percussion in a huge variety of settings. There have been the large music festivals, small theaters, big churches, little chapels, music seminars in every kind of venue, and both studio and live recording sessions—all within the last year. While I think of the vast differences in all of these situations, there are still some essentials of worship drumming that have really come to my attention. Even after all these years of playing in ministry situations, they seem to be as important to me as ever. I guess you could say they are the pillars of a worship drummer's life. These are the four elements that will always need to be in place if we are going to be at our best in our playing and our calling.

- Heart and soul
- Timing and groove
- Team spirit
- Playing to the room

I know there are many concepts, both technically and spiritually, that we use to play the drums in worship. That's really the focus of this book. You'll hear me emphasize this primary theme to learning throughout these writings. Growing as a worship musician is both a technical and spiritual journey. But these "big four" are really the corner tent pegs that hold it all together. Two are spiritual in nature, and the other two are technical. I don't think anyone would be surprised by me saying that. But honestly, that was not deliberate on my part. It just seemed to be obvious to me as I pondered this subject. I think everything else rests on these principles. All that I have ever shared and taught on the subject of drums in worship seem to be built on these four essentials. When any of them are out of place, it seems the whole thing falls down!

Heart and Soul

"You gotta' have heart—lots and lots and lots of heart." These words from an old song still have the most profound meaning. As a musician, if you are not fully engaged in the emotions of the music you're playing, it will feel lifeless. I believe that the passion and purpose you feel in worship is felt by your fellow minstrels and the people listening. Playing with great *feel* or *soul* is an accepted term in every genre of music, but usually no one is able to pinpoint exactly what is meant by it.

This concept is a little difficult to describe in technical terms. Do we hit harder or lighter? Is it the expression on our face? I don't think so. But it is something inside of us, as musicians, that is an emotional response to the music we're playing. I can only testify to my own experience and struggles with staying engaged emotionally with music. I just know that the music feels different when I'm aware of what I am supposed to communicate, and that I am excited to tell the story. Yes, we have to play it like we mean it! When my heart isn't in it, there is energy or an emotion that is lacking. I think that is the soul part of music. And people are sensitive to it even when they are not focused on that aspect of listening to music. They still feel the music, because it is a language of the soul!

Raising the Bar for Worship

This is even more critical when it comes to worship. We must be worshipping when we play. It has to be more than getting the notes right. Playing with skill and excellence is great to a certain level, but there is a realm of spiritual power that will only happen when we are playing to honor and love the Lord. The times I have been disengaged emotionally during a performance, it felt rather lame. The word *performance* in this situation is only being used to refer to a time of playing. Some people in ministry situations do not like using that word.

I don't use it to mean promoting ourselves as musicians. In worship we should never think of exalting ourselves, which is so often the normal mind-set of musicians on a stage.

Figure 2.1. Carl in worship.

Again, to specifically describe what is lacking in those moments when we just don't care as much about what we're doing is tough. I truly believe that the music is lifeless in some way, and everyone suffers because of it. It's so much like how we relate to people that we either love or dislike. Music really does have that much emotional power. This brings me to the first of four conceptual pillars that I believe set the tone for worshippers—specifically worship drummers—to remain in a good place to serve the worship team and the church. Guard your heart!

"Thou shalt not play the drums in vain!"

It's Gotta Groove!

Your sense of time and groove must be solid. This is the technical side of your playing. As much as your heart being in it is vital, so is your ability to do the job well. Yes, we want it to be an excellent performance.

Keep working on your chops (your skill)! Make sure you have every song worked out thoroughly. Don't just guess at how a song is supposed to be played. Act as if the drum part is a composed piece of music, and that way you'll pay more attention to the details. If you know there are spots in a tune that are challenging you, work on it some more. You might have to slow a section down to figure out a drum fill or groove pattern, but that's okay. Playing a section slower just allows you to put it under the musical microscope and work out the details. This technique lets your body and mind coordinate the feel of the groove better. It helps in building what we call "muscle memory."

Using a metronome when you practice is most critical. Playing along with the music in your headphones is a great way to learn the song and really get into it. But you should also turn it off and play with the click at the song tempo and just play it from memory. This will show you where something might need a little more work. Playing with a recording covers up your flaws, and you don't want them to show up later when it's just you playing the drums with your band. The drummer on the record won't be there to cover for you. There will be more about clicks and metronomes in another chapter.

Keeping the time solid and the groove feeling great is *primo*! Don't be content with anything less than your absolute best. But don't get caught up in self-destructive thoughts either. Thoughts such as "I wish I could play like that drummer" or "I'll never be able to get this right!" are destructive.

It's okay to be inspired by other players, but always remember, "Thou shalt not covet thy neighbor's drumming; just keep the groove solid!"

Be a Team Player

Team spirit is the next pillar for a great worship musician. By the way, remember that each element is vital. Just because I'm using a particular order does not mean I'm placing more significance on one area.

Besides having your act together on the spiritual and technical side, you have to help your teammates as well. Ah... you thought this would be easy. No way! Now, you also have to build up your fellow worship warriors.

When you're feeling strong, look for those who are not having a good day, and encourage them. Actually, we need to do this whether we feel good or not. Rise above your emotions! I know this is challenging, because I have to do this too from time to time. It could be something very small in your own eyes. Just a kind word or maybe helping the team set up can change the atmosphere. The ordinary things can have such a huge impact. Look for ways to build people up, and you'll find it becomes the emotional and spiritual glue that holds you all together.

Figure 2.2. Pulling together before a concert. Greg Bissonette, Abe Laboriel, Tom Brooks, Will McFarlane, Kirk Whalum, and Carl.

If you feel there is a spiritual void and no one is giving much attention to prayer and heart issues, you might be the one to draw the team into fellowship time. Don't be a nag, but encourage the troops to gather in for a focused time before an event to meet with the Lord in prayer. Like great sports teams have a locker room gathering before a game, a worship team has got to pull together in the final moments before a service. Oh, by the way, ask the leader if it's okay. Don't just take over the role of leadership. Always strive to be the encourager!

Here's pillar three. "Thou shalt honor your brothers and sisters."

Play to the Room

Be sure to play to the room your band is performing in. Yes, this means to control your volume. Everything else could be in place, but if you overpower the room, it will weaken all the other pillars. And for the drummer, this is the greatest musical challenge in every situation. You could be a great musician with incredible skill, have the passion to worship, and totally be the team player, but if you don't adjust to the acoustic environment you're in, you've failed. Usually this means being too loud, but on rare occasions, you might be playing too softly to get the band to sound good together. Sometimes you have to dig in a little bit to get the band to gel. But normally, overplaying or playing too loudly is the problem.

I've experienced this many times on tours around the world. One night we'll play a huge amphitheater and I can play as hard as I want. The very next night, we're in a smaller indoor venue with terrible acoustics, and I have to play the whole evening with Hot Rods and lighter sticks. Theaters, churches, small meeting rooms, and huge outdoor arenas all require a different approach in my playing. Even though the drums are miked up and being projected through a PA system, how things really feel is affected by the live volume I produce onstage next to the other players. I always work with the engineer and the whole team to be sure we sound as good as we can for whatever room we play. We'll discuss more in-depth volume issues later.

Just remember pillar four, "Thou shalt not kill the worship atmosphere."

So you say, "Hey, Carl, that's only four; I thought there were Ten Commandments." Hey! Yo! Give me a break! I'm not Moses here! Sheeesh! I did not get these ideas from two stone tablets! Anyway, enough of the cheesy humor. The point I'm trying to make is that these four pillars are really the primary things that come to mind when I'm playing. Every job seems to lean upon these concepts. All the other elements of being a great worship drummer rest on these four. At every conference or clinic, these are the most discussed topics among players, worship leaders, and pastors. Really! I'm being dramatic on purpose. You have to get this!! Make these the cornerstones of your calling, and you'll truly be the drummer the Lord has called you to be.

- Thou shalt not play the drums in vain.
- Thou shalt not covet thy neighbor's drumming; just keep the groove solid.
- Thou shalt honor your brothers and sisters.
- Thou shalt not kill the worship atmosphere.

3

Bring Joy to the Music

Figure 3.1. Carl with Paul Jackson Jr., Abe Laboriel, and Tom Brooks.

As we played, we cried. I don't even remember the song at this point. I just remember seeing Abe's face decorated with tears of joy. The worship was powerful, and the music flowed with the move of the Spirit. As he turned to look back at me on the drums, we smiled, knowing the Lord was truly "inhabiting the praises of His people." It felt as if the bass and drums, as well as the whole team, were in total unison. As we left the stage after that wonderful time of worship, I can vividly recall Abe Laboriel's words to me. "Brother Carl, we were laying flowers at the feet of Jesus." I could not have described the feeling better.

Something happens beyond playing the "right notes," when musicians make a sound "as one." Playing well together as a team is fun, but when your heart and soul are united in the holy pursuit of the Lord, something unique and powerful is released. A language of the spirit is being spoken. A door is opened to the throne room of God.

In these moments, I'm not thinking of being a drummer. My heart is totally focused on being in the presence of the Lord. Maybe it's the same experience the musicians had in the ancient temple when they made "a sound as with one voice." The glory of God came into that place.

> *The trumpeters and singers joined in unison, as with one voice, to give praise and thanks to the Lord. Accompanied by trumpets, cymbals, and other instruments, they raised their voices in praise to the Lord and sang: "He is good; his love endures forever." Then the temple of the Lord was filled with a cloud, and the priests could not perform their service because of the cloud, for the glory of the Lord filled the temple of God.*
>
> —II Chronicles 5:13–14

Others Sense Your Passion

I don't remember if someone told me the story or if I read it somewhere, but Abe Laboriel Jr. (the drummer/son of Abe Sr., the bass player) told pop-music icon Sting, "I want to bring joy to your music." Sting had just seen Abe Jr. perform at a festival date with another artist. He was so impressed, he asked him to be part of his band. Abe Jr. got the gig.

Abe Jr. played for Sting for a season like he had for many other artists through the years. Currently he tours with Paul McCartney. Every time I see him play, I witness him bringing joy to the music. He makes me laugh sometimes. The same way his father makes me laugh with joy when we play music together. I've learned from them, as well as from other joyful, exciting musicians, to play passionately at all times. It's as if they would be dishonoring the gift the Lord had given them if they did not give themselves fully to the music they are bringing to life. I've even heard great players say, "If you don't mean it, don't play it."

There are times we all feel out of it. I have played many times when I was exhausted, emotionally drained, or even when I was very ill. Through the years, I've also done my share of playing carelessly with no passion. But now I rarely, if ever, sit at the drums and do not give myself fully to the music before me. Especially in playing for praise and worship, there seems to be a heightened awareness of the responsibility to the calling of a minstrel. And I truly believe that embracing my musicianship as a calling has molded me into the player that I am now. It feels stronger and more passionate now than it did 30 years ago when I started playing professionally.

It's the Soul That Matters

It's not a matter of more notes being played or my technique becoming more refined. If anything, I'm probably playing fewer notes now in a song than I ever have before. Well, that depends on the style of music I'm playing and the creative desires of the artist. But in general, it feels like every note counts more. As if each one has meaning. And they do!

All great musicians I know make the most out of every sound they make. We might say they have *soul* or a *deep feel* to their playing.

So you may be wondering, am I talking about "soul" in playing music, or is this a discussion of technical excellence? I believe this is definitely a soul or heart issue. Technique seems to have little bearing here.

The variety of styles and techniques of playing an instrument seem to be limitless. I've witnessed many great players with very different styles. Some actually looked like they were playing all wrong. Or so I thought. They would use totally unorthodox techniques, but the sound and power of the music would be indescribable. There is something about being "into the music" that charges the atmosphere. A musician that gives an emotional, soulful performance seems to impact people deeply. People feel moved. Their souls or emotions have been touched.

Figure 3.2. Carl deep in the moment.

My Steve Gadd Experience

I recently attended a Steve Gadd clinic in the Nashville area. He spent the afternoon at a local drum shop meeting fans and signing autographs. I had the chance to shake his hand and get a picture. Few words were spoken. I just thanked him for being an inspiration to me. In a very quiet and peaceful tone, he just humbly thanked me for my kind words. That evening at the clinic, in front of hundreds of fans, he played some beautiful drum solos. But what shocked me the most was that as he played, my heart was moved and I felt like crying. I wasn't some starstruck groupie, like Steve is some kind of movie star, so I asked the Lord what that was about. This was not a worship event, but I was really moved in my spirit. In my heart, I felt the Lord say, "I have anointed Steve to play."

Wow! I don't know what Steve's relationship is with the Lord, but his gifting is powerful. And that night, the Lord made it clear that it was His (God's) anointing and gifting in Steve that empowered his playing.

Is it true of all gifts the Lord gives mankind? I feel it is. In fact I believe all skill and talent is from God. Even when people don't honor or acknowledge the Lord in their lives, His gifts are still displayed in His creation. For those great talents that are not following God, I refer to them as "the lost tribe of Levites." That's pretty wild, isn't it? But think of the many inspiring artists you've seen or heard, and I think you'll understand where I'm coming from.

Moving around a lot, making faces, and other outward expressions are not necessarily a sign of a musician's passion. That can all be learned as performance technique. Sometimes a player can just look intense, serious, or thoughtful. Although I think some sign of emotion should be happening when you are playing. I mean, if music is a language of the soul and you're expressing yourself, people should see some sign of life! Music should create a reaction in your heart, not just your head. Even more so in the experience we have as minstrels expressing ourselves to the Lord.

The Worship Effect

I feel my deepest emotions in praise and worship. Although as a professional musician, something always stirs my heart when I'm playing beautiful music. And I'm purposely not defining a style. I think you know the point I'm making, if you've felt the same way when playing music you really enjoy. If you don't feel anything when you play, prayerfully consider what you are doing. Maybe being a musician is not the Lord's call on your life. I don't mean the occasional slump. I'm talking about the sense of never having an emotional reaction to what you're playing. If there is no joy or passion in it, let it go! Like Eric Liddell, the 1924 Olympic runner whose story was told in the movie *Chariots of Fire*, said, "When I run, I feel God's pleasure." You should also feel the Lord's pleasure when you are doing what He made you for.

When I'm playing drums and percussion, there's a sense of peace and joy that comes over me. I really do feel the pleasure of the Lord. I also have a sense that He meets me there with some divine purpose. When I pour myself into the gift the Lord has given me, He's giving something back. We might call that the anointing. The Lord being with us or blessing us when we play.

> *The Lord is with him.*
>
> —I Samuel 16:18

It is a special anointing to play sounds that lead people in praise and worship. This is also the empowering to break spiritual bondages or cast out demons. In the Old Testament, when David played for King Saul, it says that even the evil spirits would leave.

> *David would take his harp and play. Then relief would come to Saul; he would feel better, and the evil spirit would leave him.*
>
> —I Samuel 16:23

Maybe it's just the Lord's manifest presence being released when we play to honor Him. The Word says in Psalm 22:3 that the Lord "inhabits or is enthroned on the praises of His people (Israel)." And I believe He does! Take some time to read that from different translations of the Bible, and be inspired by what that really means for us as worshippers of God.

So is this something we can learn, like we do a new lick or drum groove? In a way, I think so. By pursuing the Lord and being mentored by other minstrels who understand their Godly anointing, we can grow into our deeper calling. I think I always knew there was something stirring in my heart about being a drummer, but it took years to understand what this passion is that I have for the instrument. This passionate pursuit of the Lord goes beyond just being a musician. It affects my whole life. Have I perfected it? Not at all, but I've embraced the journey.

Some Spiritual Exercises

You might be thinking, "Okay, Carl, give me something practical to work on." Well, if you know you were made to be a musician and it is your passion, then you can begin here. For starters, I always sing along with the songs, or at least learn the words. I want to know the meaning of what I'm playing. Let me remind you, this isn't about thinking every song is great. It's about you knowing the heart of the song and injecting life into it. When you play drums for others, the life of their music depends on your heart being engaged. "Bring joy to the music."

Another "soul exercise" I use is to pray when I play. When I'm practicing, I'll start to pray and then play a solo and just let the music pour out of my heart. Don't analyze what you're doing. Just get before the Lord. Literally picture Him listening to the music you are creating and think of the Lord smiling. Be the "Little Drummer Boy" (or girl) and just play for Him. I think you'll be amazed at what happens. You might feel your spirit stirring. If not, don't be discouraged; just play from your heart, and don't think about performing or your analyzing your skill or anything technical. Just pray and play!

Start to apply these simple soul exercises to whatever musical situation you are in. I believe you will see and hear a difference. I wouldn't be surprised if others comment on how good the music feels or that the worship seems more powerful or richer to them. And finally, don't forget to stay humble before the Lord and realize that He is releasing something deeper and more passionate into you and into your music.

Rejoice in the Lord always, again I say, rejoice!

—Philippians 4:4

Figure 3.3. Playing in worship is a joy!

Bring joy to the music!

4

Playing to the Room: A Drummer's Perspective

Let's talk further about the challenge of adjusting your playing style and volume to the acoustics of a venue. The most common and controversial statement drummers hear is, "Can you play softer?" Drum volume is one of the biggest issues with bands, especially in church and ministry settings. It is the most controversial because opinions are very strong concerning expressing yourself musically and spiritually while trying to keep the volume lower. Musicians often feel like they're being stifled by the restrictions that are placed on them because of the acoustic environments they deal with. Well today, my friends, I will give you the answer to this problem: stop playing drums! Of course I'm just kidding, so let's talk.

I've discussed dynamics and decibels briefly in other writings, but we'll cover them in greater detail now. Especially since I am continually bombarded with questions about this issue at seminars, on tour, and in the online forums. This is a big topic!

Everyone Has to Adjust

Ultimately all musicians should adjust to the situation they are working in and have the attitude of making the whole band sound great. Guitar and bass amps along with loud monitors can wreak havoc on controlling the decibel level onstage. It's pretty simple to deal with amp volume problems. You can simply turn down, try turning it to a different angle, put it in an amp box, or even remove it from the stage and put it in a backstage closet. In the modern musical production world, we have a lot of options.

The drummer's job is particularly difficult, because, by nature, drums are acoustically a loud instrument. We can't just turn them down, and I think it's a little weird to put the drums backstage. So let's work with changing the instrument you use.

Shrinking the Drum Kit

The first solution in making the drum kit quieter is to use smaller drums and cymbals. A 20-inch kick is more focused and punchy sounding than a larger kick drum. I know it changes the tone and fatness of the kick sound. But actually a smaller bass drum is very powerful in a smaller room. At my home church we have several kits, and I actually prefer the one with the smaller kick. It just seems to work better in the gymnasium where we meet.

Figure 4.1. Smaller kick drum on the church kit.

The standard tom-tom sizes of 12- and 13-inch rack toms, and a 16-inch floor tom, could be downsized to a 10-, 12-, and 14-inch tom setup. In the photo of our church kit, we're using a 20-inch kick, 12-, 14-, and 16-inch toms, a 14-inch by 6 1/2-inch main snare, a 14-inch by 5-inch side snare, and a djembe. The lower physical mass of material that you have in your kit will actually lower the volume of the drums themselves. Be aware that, as we discuss these options, you still have to control how hard you hit the drums. It all works together.

The snare drum I prefer is a 14-inch diameter by 5-inch deep brass model. It is really the perfect all-purpose snare in my opinion. Larger snares in general are going to sound thick acoustically and project more decibels overall. Smaller snares are going to be too bright and snappy. A brass snare has the best of both worlds. Because brass is heavy it has warmth, and because it's metal it also has enough brightness to cut through all of the other sounds of a modern band adequately. For the rest of the kit, maple drums sound beautiful, but they do tend to be louder and have more resonance than other material. You may switch to birch or other woods that will not sound as dense or massive. Believe me, a smaller kit really does project less volume, but as I've said, you still have to control your dynamics. There will be more on this later.

Don't Forget the Cymbals

The same theory applies to cymbals. Smaller and lighter-weight cymbals will project less volume. I use a 20-inch medium ride, 16-, 17-, and 18-inch medium-thin crashes, 8- and 12-inch splash cymbals, and 14-inch medium hi-hats for most situations. They are a mixture of Meinl cymbals from their Amun and Byzance series. I may change things a little according to the music I'm working on, but I start with this setup. No big rock model or heavy cymbals. I only use them when the job requires it. And that is not usually the case in most churches.

Figure 4.2. My basic cymbal setup, adding an 18-inch China crash.

Even in more modern designed churches that are built with concert sound in mind, I would choose a smaller setup like I'm talking about. I like to let the engineer work on getting a great mix with an awesome-sounding kit rather than thinking I need to project more volume into the room. My goal as a drummer is to make the kit sound balanced as I play. I don't want one particular element to stand out dynamically unless the music requires it. The person mixing sound always notices this balanced drum sound. I try especially to be mindful not to hit the cymbals too hard. It's very easy to hear bright cymbals overpower the rest of the kit or even be picked up a lot by the vocal mics if the singers are close to the drums. Only for arena tours do I think of using bigger drum kits. But even in that situation, I try to keep my volume consistent across all elements of the kit.

Drum Enclosures Are Sometimes Necessary

You may be playing a smaller kit and trying to play softly, but it never seems to be quiet enough. Even using smaller sticks, Hot Rods, or brushes doesn't seem to give you a low enough volume. This is most often the situation in churches that are very traditional in design and culture, and then try to make the transition to using a band rather than just organ or piano. It's not always the drums being too loud that is really the issue, but the psychological effect of seeing a band setup in a classic old sanctuary. Unfortunately most of these old venues are not drum friendly. This is simply because of the acoustics of the room. Hard floors, brick walls, and lots of windows are not helpful to the acoustic challenges of a modern worship band. And the most offensive instrument is normally the drum kit.

Another thing you can do to get the volume of the kit down is to set up on a nice padded rug. A bare floor reflects sound too much, and a rug will help control it. Be sure its design looks good onstage; your band and the congregation will appreciate that. Try *not* to set up in a corner if at all possible. It acts like a megaphone for the drums. If you must do that, try to hang a theater curtain or heavy cloth on the walls around the back of the kit, and even across the back wall or area where the whole band sets up if you can cover that much area. As a last resort, build a booth for your drums, or order one from the ClearSonic company (www.clearsonic.com) or Phoenix Drum Enclosures (http://whiteleysolutions.com). If necessary you can totally enclose the drums. You can match the color and décor of the auditorium, and everyone will be happy with the sound and the look.

Figure 4.3. A ClearSonic drum enclosure.

If you use a shield or a booth, be sure to make it large enough so you can still walk around the drums. It should also be at least 2 feet higher than your highest cymbal. A drum kit must breathe or move the airwaves freely to sound its best. If the booth is too small, the drums will sound choked and harsh. You can compare the sound differences by doing this little test: Try holding your open hand in front of your mouth while you are speaking, and then gradually move it away. Notice how your tone sounds warmer as you allow more space between your mouth and hand. Drums have a similar response in a booth.

Figure 4.4. A booth too close to the kit—no walking room around the drums.

There's no use putting up a short or small shield either. It will only cut down 5 to 10 percent of the decibel level, if that. If you are going to go to all of this effort and expense, then do it completely. You could possibly start in phases. Maybe begin with just the front panels. Add the back to it if that's not enough. Then the last step would be a top if necessary. Also be sure to use the sound-isolating foam inside of the glass about 3 feet high. This will give additional isolation and cut down on the harsh frequencies that reflect off of the glass.

Playing Softer May Be Required

If a booth is not an option because of expense or aesthetics, then you have to physically control your volume. Remember: playing louder does not make you more spiritual or dramatic. In fact there's a joke that goes something like this:

A person asks the drummer, "Can you play with some dynamics?"

The drummer says, "What do you mean? I'm playing as loud as I can!"

Unfortunately many drummers think that loud means passionate or dynamic. But really volume has nothing to do with it. What's in your heart when you play is what matters. So be able to play at whatever volume level is needed for the room you are in, and play passionately always.

In your stick bag should be many different sizes and weights of sticks, brushes, mallets, Hot Rods, and so forth. Your favorite standard-size stick should be plentiful. For me that favorite stick is a Vater 5A, nylon tip. Use heavier sticks for big outdoor events or other loud situations, and very light jazz sticks for smaller rooms. Hot Rods by Pro Mark or Splashsticks by Vater are excellent for keeping your volume down and still hearing some snap when you play. Even have the lighter Blasticks or Ultraflex brushes for those supersoft settings. I even keep a few odd items in my stick collection for special effects. The kitchen is a great place to find interesting drum tools.

Figure 4.5. Assorted mallets, sticks, brushes, chopsticks, and egg beaters in my stick bag.

I always hear drummers say that it doesn't sound as cool or real when they use lighter sticks, rods, or brushes. My response is that they are correct in saying it sounds different, but that has nothing to do with being cool. Sometimes playing really soft is cool. I'm not sure that is even the goal in modern worship, but I understand where they're coming from. Yes, the tone is different. But it's sometimes the adjustment we have to make for the music to really blend in a difficult room.

Techniques for Softer Volumes

The key is to find the right technique on the drums and cymbals when you use other tools. Sometimes I'll play with a little more snap when using brushes or rods. I might also experiment with where I hit the drums or how I make a rim shot just to get the right sound. Approach this as a challenge, not as a handicap. It will add to your creativity if you choose to make it so.

It's also very important to practice everything you do at a variety of dynamic levels. Use a metronome to play all of the songs and exercises you are working on. While you do that, switch to every type of stick, brush, mallet, and bundlestix you have in your bag. Make it feel great with anything you pick up. Even your bare hands! You'll be amazed how versatile you will become.

Adjusting the height of your stroke when you are playing will definitely affect your volume. Practice until you are comfortable playing very high strokes for louder volume, using a lot of wrist and arm action, as well as low strokes for soft playing, just barely raising the sticks off of the drums. At the softer dynamic levels, be sure to use more finger control and less wrist action. It may take time to get your soft playing under control if you have been playing loud for a long time. Be patient and keep practicing it. And yes, with the metronome!

Be aware of the dynamics of your feet as well. Your kick drum volume will have to be in balance with the rest of the kit, although in most popular music, the kick is played harder as compared to jazz styles. The main thing is for you to develop your control for whatever setting you are playing in. The hi-hat foot will probably not be as critical, but be attentive to it as well.

Electronic Drums

I know that many of you have played electronic or digital drums to solve the volume problem. That's a great idea if there are no options to make your real drums work in the situation you're in. The new technology is really amazing for digital drums. It's much better now than in the early days of the hard trigger pads and poor-sounding samples. Roland, Yamaha,

Ddrums, and others are all making fantastic instruments. Drum sampling has improved immensely, and the latest pads feel as natural as possible without actually playing real drums.

But They Sounded So Good at the Store

If you play a digital kit, be sure the PA system in your auditorium or church can handle all the extra channels and reproduce the sound evenly throughout the venue. That is a big concern in churches, and it usually is the prime reason for not switching to electric drums. Unfortunately, many drummers and music directors fail to take that into consideration when trying out digital drums in a music store. They sounded great in the small show room or in the headphones you used, but they sound weak in the auditorium. So be sure to thoroughly analyze the sound system in your venue before deciding to try digital drums. Play some drum-dominant music in the PA, and walk around the room to hear if the system is covering the room well and that drum sounds are clear in every area.

For monitoring, you should use headphones or earbuds onstage. I rarely use speakers for monitoring anymore. Even when I'm playing acoustic drums, I still prefer to use in-ear monitors. It normally sounds better, and it helps in controlling stage volume. You can have the mix just the way you like it without overpowering the other players. Be aware that you still have to control your dynamics according to the venue. Sometimes using headphones can cause a drummer to play too loudly. Ask the engineer how you're blending in the room with the rest of the band.

I would also use the small drum or keyboard amps they make for digital drum setups for the band to hear the kit on the platform. But this should not be used to project your drum sound into the room. So don't get carried away with the volume.

Even though you're trying to reduce your volume, the drums still must blend in and feel like part of the music onstage. I usually put the amp on one side of my electric setup with an extension speaker on the opposite side. This creates the sense that there is a real drum kit on the platform. I've even heard singers complain about digital drums having no life onstage. They may not have wanted the drums to be too loud, but they wanted to feel something grooving behind them. Using amps and microphones is not to make your drums louder than other musicians, but to create a musical blend and give them definition in the room.

Even when playing a great digital drum kit, I still add a real snare to the left of the hi-hat pad. I also add a few real cymbals and some percussion toys for those moments when

I want to do something really delicate. But I won't use the real acoustic instruments for any loud hits. That is reserved for the electronic pads.

Remember that our job as drummers is to create a strong musical and spiritual foundation so everyone can enjoy what's happening. Our focus is to serve the Lord and the people with the skills He has placed in us. It's all for His glory! Now go play softly, and this time *with feeling*!

5

These Are the Best Drums

I'm about to reveal to you the greatest set of drums I've ever played. Without a doubt, I know these drums will blow away any other drum kit out there. Don't even try to change my mind on this, because I've played every kind of set of drums made in the world. All of the greatest drummers play them too. Okay, ready? The best drums ever are $#@!#!#@#!$. What! You say you couldn't hear me? I said, $#@!#@!$#@!$#. They really are amazing. You must get them, or you're just not the most hip, cool, up-to-date, stylin' cat out there—like all of the other really happenin' drummers who play these drums.

Okay, okay, stop! For those of you that know me, you know I don't get into these kinds of discussions. There is no greatest drum set ever. I've even worked in several drum shops through the years, and this was always part of the common shoptalk. "Oh, man, you should really get these!" or "What! You've never played those drums? They're the best! You're really missing it, dude." It didn't take long for me to realize that the art of drumming is much more than what drum set you play. In all honesty, every manufacturer is making great drums.

Play What You Love

My favorite equipment recommendation is to play what you love and what inspires you. It doesn't matter if it's Yamaha, Pearl, Tama, DW, Gretsch, or any of the other great drums out there. Play the drums that make you want to play! What drums inspire you? When you play "that" drum kit, then you've found your instrument. And don't let anyone mess with your head about it.

What makes drums sound great is a great player making great music with other great performers when everything technically comes together. Now I admit that can be a very complicated thing, but let's stay focused on the drum issue. We could also talk about cymbals, sticks, drumheads, and so forth, but again, we will stay in drum world for now.

In all drum making, even with custom-built drums, there are some concepts that apply to everyone. I know there are a thousand variations in the small details, but we'll focus on the big issues. Types of wood, the sizes, the rims, and the tom-mounting system of the kit are probably the biggest factors of drum sound. And this isn't even discussing the electronic and engineering options.

Types of Wood Shells

First, all maple drums will probably be the premier item in every company's catalog. I happen to play a Yamaha Maple Custom Absolute series kit with aluminum die-cast hoops. I use a 22-inch kick; 10-, 12-, 14-, and 16-inch toms with all standard depth measurements; and a 14-inch by 5-inch maple snare. I do have other kits and about 15 snares, but this is my primary setup. Yes, I think they're awesome, and have been thrilled with the sound they create. But every maple kit has very similar characteristics. They all sound big! Maple shells project and resonate more than others. Listen to Paul Baloche's projects: *A Greater Song* and *Our God Saves*. That's the kit I used on both of those. It's the kit I prefer in the studio and for live events. I may choose different sizes according to the gig, but this drum kit can really cover all the bases. And they inspire me. I love to play these drums.

Figure 5.1. My personal Yamaha kit.

Maple in general is a very hard wood, but it is also very resonant. I don't know all of the technical reasons, but they are punchy and have a lot of tone. In some settings, maple drums can be a little too big sounding. I've heard some people say the sound spreads out too much, and that they keep ringing too long. So if you want a slightly more focused, tight sound, maybe you should try birch or other drums. I just muffle my drums more if the producer or engineer asks me to do so.

Birch drums, like the classic Yamaha Recording Custom series, are amazing too. These drums were the early sound of Steve Gadd, Dave Weckl, Paul Leim, and others. They have a little more midrange in tone and a little tighter punch. Now does that mean better? No, it's just different. Especially when it comes to the sound of the toms. Many players like Gadd and Leim are using maple kick drums with birch toms. This would give you a huge, fat-sounding kick, with toms that are a little punchier in the midrange.

All the drum companies would advertise and price their maple and birch kits as the top-of-the-line drums. Beyond that they would start to use other types of wood and combinations of them, perhaps combining these popular woods with mahogany or oak or others. If you are reading drum magazines and catalogs, you probably find the variations pretty overwhelming. But honestly, what I've observed is that when you get into the less expensive drums, they all sound more controlled and not as resonant. Which is not necessarily a bad thing. In some settings, you don't want the drums to sound so huge. If you play in smaller venues all of the time, a less resonant kit might work better. I've used Yamaha Oak Custom drums or other inexpensive kits that sounded awesome, but they just didn't sound as big. In general the cheaper kits don't seem to create as much volume. The key in most settings is tuning and head selection, which I will discuss more later.

Use Your Own Kit Design

You could really put together whatever kind of drum kit you could imagine with the current list of options that are available, although I personally like to hear a drum kit with the same tonal characteristics across all of the drums. Of course, next week I could change my mind. Remember, this is art!

Besides types of wood, there are also variations in size and thickness of shell we could choose from. Deeper drums will sound fatter and maybe darker. Shorter drums will be punchier. Thinner shells will sound brighter than thicker shells, and so on. If the drums have die-cast hoops rather than machined steel, they will probably have more of a snap or cutting sound.

The best way to tune your ear to these variations in sound is to go to a shop and try a lot of different drums. Don't be a pest, but ask the store salespeople if you can take some time to try things out. Try out everything, and take mental note of what make and model you're playing. Be sensitive to the workers and customers, and try to do your testing in minutes and not hours of playing in a store. I think you'll get excited as you discover what sounds inspire you. It's amazing to play drums and feel that connection to a sound.

Always keep in mind what you'll be using the kit for. Are you recording? Are you playing in mostly large rooms or small? Is the music more rock, pop, or jazz, or is it a combination of everything? Of course you may feel you need more options, but you don't have the budget or space to own several sets of drums. So how can you pick out a kit that will work for everything? In general, the standard kit I mentioned earlier really does cover all of the bases. It's a big investment up front, but it will last a lifetime if you take care of it.

If I'm playing in smaller venues, I might only use the three smaller toms, use a smaller snare, and put more padding in the kick. When I don't have to worry about the room, I use everything and let them ring. I muffle as little as possible most of the time. Drums have a voice, and I like to let them speak. Again this is always subject to what the job calls for.

No matter what type of kit I use, I look for the tom mountings to be some kind of suspension system. Even on a cheap kit, this can make all the difference in the resonance of the toms and how easily they will tune. Mountings that attach to or go through the shell will usually distort the sound or decrease its resonance. Quite often I can't get these types of drums to tune properly or resonate well. Unless you want that "old school" tom sound, you have to have isolation mounting for the toms. This feature has become very standardized in modern drum manufacturing and can be found on even the cheapest of drum sets.

I hope this helps keep your mind at ease if you've been wondering if your drums aren't the best drums in the world. Or maybe this will help you in your journey if you have been thinking of a change in kits. Again, try out a lot of drums and get your ears tuned in to what's out there.

You might just add some pieces. Maybe smaller toms or a smaller kick drum would be a good change if you're in a small room. It could be that a cheaper, less resonant kit is more suitable to your situation. Buying a really loud, top-of-the-line kit and putting a lot of muffling on everything is a terrible waste of money.

If you would like to, let me know how it's going in your journey in discovering the sound of drums. You can write to my e-mail or the forum on my website: www.carlalbrecht.com. Happy drum hunting! Oh, and remember: don't worry about finding the best drums in the world. I think they're in heaven with Buddy Rich. Ha!

6

Choosing Cymbals

Finding the right cymbals for your style of playing can be one of the most challenging and frustrating tasks for a drummer. With so many options, you might feel it's like trying to find your favorite tree in the forest. You end up with that feeling of being totally lost in the woods. Well come along with me and let's go cymbal hunting. I've walked this trail before.

Let's first decide what you want to accomplish. Do you need cymbals for a heavy rock band or a jazz trio? Is your style more Latin or classical? If you're playing in a contemporary worship setting, maybe you just want a great all-purpose set of cymbals to do everything.

I would definitely recommend having a set of cymbals that will cover all the bases. This is very important if you are just starting to build your collection. Whether you're a beginner or an experienced drummer, don't think of getting weird "special effects" or "style designed" cymbals if your budget is limited. Look for a good ride cymbal, a couple of crashes, a splash, and a great set of hi-hats. You can add to your collection later, but use this as a starting point.

Figure 6.1. Carl's start-up cymbal set.

Who Makes the Best Cymbals?

Which company makes the best cymbals? To be honest, all of the major cymbal companies are making great instruments. And they all offer a large variety of cymbals to choose from. So just like with drum kits, I say, "Play what inspires you." I personally prefer Meinl cymbals. I am also aware of what the other manufacturers are making. I just happen to be very happy with what I'm hearing from Meinl.

Here is what I look for in a "general purpose" set of cymbals: they have to sound good in all the styles of music I'm playing, so they can't stand out individually or have a tone that is identified with a certain style.

For instance, in jazz the cymbals are often lighter and sound dry and dark. In rock music they are usually heavier and sound cutting and harsh. That's not always the case, but just a general reference. So in my all-purpose setup, the cymbals are medium to medium-thin weight. And the sizes are what would be considered the current standard. A 20-inch medium ride; 18-, 17-, or 16-inch medium to medium-thin crashes; an 8-inch and 12-inch splash; and 14-inch medium hi-hats. This is what I call the modern standard package.

I normally use the Byzance series from Meinl. There are times I mix things up a bit, but that's where I start. The Byzance series sounds great in every situation. They are very similar to the classic A series from Zildjian. You could probably compare that to the AA series from Sabian or the Signature line of Paiste cymbals. All of these models are the top of the line for each of the companies I mentioned. And along with that comes the top-of-the-line price. When buying cymbals, you cannot cut corners. I recommend buying fewer pieces and getting better ones if your budget is tight. When buying drums, you can spend a little less money and still get a great sound with good heads and proper tuning. Cymbals are a whole different story. So with the setup I've listed, you could easily spend $1,500 or more.

Try Before You Buy

To save money, you could buy used cymbals, but be sure to test and inspect them carefully. Hold them up to a light, and look for any small cracks. Be sure to check the center hole for any key holing or cracks. This splitting or grinding out of the center hole happens from not keeping a nylon sleeve on the stem of the cymbal stand. You can look for sales at your local drum shop, or shop online. There are some great websites that have tons of drums and cymbals to choose from. Take your time, and don't feel pressured to buy.

If this adventure is new for you, ask the salesperson to show you a large variety of cymbals to try out. Most drum shops will have a room where you can play every cymbal that's for sale. If a store will not let you test cymbals, don't buy from it. You wouldn't buy a car without test-driving it. But don't abuse the privilege either. Once you've played a cymbal for a while, move on to another. You should be able to hear pretty quickly what sounds you like or dislike.

How to Test Cymbals

So what are we listening for? We want to find a set of cymbals that sound good as an ensemble, not just great individual instruments. I play a cymbal all over its full surface. I hit it on the bell, on the edge, and everywhere in between. I'll tap soft rhythms and then build into pretty hard slices across the edge to hear how it sounds as a crash cymbal. Yes, even on the ride cymbal! When I hit a crash, I'll let the sound decay as long as possible and listen carefully to how the tone fades. It should have a smooth, shimmering decay. If it sounds like it's flanging or making a wave tone, I'll try something else.

When playing ride patterns, does the cymbal maintain good stick definition, or does it start to wash out? In other words, does it start to sound like a cymbal roll rather than distinct individual taps? Crash cymbals will probably do that anyway, but I try to find at least one that could be used as a ride cymbal too—maybe the 17-inch crash. Ride cymbals should definitely stay controlled. They should flow with the intensity of your playing. If you love the tone of a ride but it wants to wash out too soon, you could put a little tape on it. I've got a couple like that; they sound great, but I had to put a little tape underneath to dampen or dry them out a bit. I believe a ride cymbal should only start to wash or crash when I dig into it with the shoulder of the stick rather than just playing it with the tip of the stick.

Once I've found individual favorites, I'll set them up together. I'll play patterns on the whole set and listen carefully to see if they sound great as a group. You should notice very distinct pitches. Ride to crash, splash to crash, top hi-hat to crash, and so forth. I try to hear a broad range of tones from the set. I especially choose crashes that have very different pitches but similar timbre or character. As the sounds fade, I'll listen carefully for an odd tone: a sound that just doesn't seem to fit with the other cymbals. Sometimes you have to try a different crash, or splash, or even a ride cymbal. I know this is an art, and it takes time to learn. Just be patient, and you'll get the hang of it. That's why it's probably a good idea to try cymbals from the same series when you first do this. But after a while, you'll be able to mix and match cymbals according to what your ears are hearing and not by what you're seeing. Even with the best design and manufacturing processes, each cymbal is unique. The same models may be very close, but there are always subtle nuances that I think make each one an individual voice.

Proper Cymbal Mounting

When mounting the cymbals, be sure the plastic sleeve is on the stem of the cymbal stand and that it is in good condition. This cushions the cymbal hole and protects it against grinding. Also check the base plate on the stem. If it's curved, make sure it curves downward. It's supposed to match the shape of the bell of the cymbal. And last but not least, be sure the felt washers are in place on the bottom and top of your cymbals. All of these elements affect the tone of your cymbals. Don't tighten the wing nuts too much either. Crashes and splashes have to move freely to get the best tone. Ride cymbals can be a little tighter to control the tone if you'd like, but the general rule is to "let them breath." Even the top hi-hat should be able to wiggle so the tone is not choked. It only needs to be tight enough to track properly with your foot action. Of course you can adjust anything according to your own creative choices, but use these rules as a guide.

The angle of your cymbals is also important. No matter what height you place your cymbals at, angle them to point toward your chest. This will line them up with the motion of your arms and wrists. When crashing your cymbals, use a "slicing" stroke. Do not hit straight on the edge of your cymbals. They will not hold up under that kind of stress. All of these guidelines should give your cymbals a long life. When making this kind of investment, you'll be glad you followed these general rules.

Over time, I'm sure you'll want to add to your collection. Maybe another crash or splash would be nice. Whatever cymbal you add, be sure to do the same testing method. I used to take my ride and two crash cymbals with me to test the new one alongside them. Now my ears can pretty much hear a cymbal to identify its character and tone enough to get a good match. Remember though: this is still an art form. Don't hesitate to try different types of cymbals to expand your musical palate. A good set of cymbals will be a key element to your sound. As I said before, take your time and choose carefully.

Blessings to you, and good cymbal hunting.

7

Getting a Great Drum Sound and Other Mysteries of the Universe

Tuning drums and using the right ones for the job are among the most vital skills for a drummer. They are as important as learning how to play well. Even if you are a very skilled player, that doesn't guarantee your sound is pleasing to the artist or listener. You have to be able to adjust your sound according to the style you're playing, the feel of the band, the sound of the room, and many other factors.

There are a variety of methods to the art of getting a great drum sound. I won't claim to have the one secret formula to the best drum sound, because that is an objective thing. But I have learned a few tricks through the years that I am happy to share.

I also encourage you to try many different methods so that you know how to do different tunings and adjustments to the kit according to the sounds you want to create. Finally, beware of anyone who says you have to do it a certain way. Remember: these are supposed to be creative musical ideas, not doctrines. I've had drummers tell me "You should never do that" or "It should always be like this." Sorry, that's totally locking your creativity in a box. I agree there are some formulas to follow, but don't be afraid to experiment. Learn the rules for sure, but break the rules if necessary. So here we go. Get out your tuning key and your creativity, and let's get to work.

A Reminder About Drum Design

There are so many different drum and head designs nowadays that it can be difficult to know what you need. I am not one to argue about who makes the best gear, because all of the companies are making great products. Whether you play Yamaha, Pearl, Tama, Gretsch, or another well-respected manufacturer's drum kit, you're going to get good drum equipment. Which models or series of their drums you get has a lot to do with the sound. But with any drum kit, the head choice and tuning is a huge part of the sound. I happen to play Yamaha drums, but I've played many of the other manufacturers' stuff as well. I will use kits at the request of artists or producers as needed, and sometimes on tour, I just have to play what's available. It's actually been a great way to learn about the sound of drums. What models and sizes we use will make a difference. But I believe drumheads and tuning are a much bigger factor in the sound of a drum kit.

In general I prefer maple-shell drums with thinner plies (this relates to the layers of wood that affect the thickness of the shell) no matter what brand of drums I'm playing. They usually sound bigger and brighter than other types of wood. Although birch shells can have more midrange punch, they don't have the massive sound that maple can project. These types of kits will cost a lot. If you are on a tighter budget, all of the companies make excellent mid-price-range kits that have combinations of wood that still sound great. I usually recommend these kits if you are trying to control the volume of the drums in a difficult auditorium, like a church where you are always asked to play softer. They normally don't create the volume that top-of-the-line kits do. And as I've said before, I also suggest using smaller sizes. The normal sizes for a drum kit are as follows: 22-inch kick drum; 12-, 13-, and 16-inch tom-toms; 14-inch snare (usually about 6-inch deep). For smaller venues, try a 20-inch kick; 10-, 12-, and 14-inch toms; and keep the 14-inch snare; that size is a good, all-purpose model. You'll be amazed how good the smaller drums sound without overpowering the room.

Snare drums are a totally different animal. Maple ones sound great, but I still prefer a brass shell. Remember, brass is a heavier metal, so it still sounds warm or darker. But because it is a metal shell, it has some high tones that a wood-shell drum doesn't project. My favorite brass snare is the Yamaha 14 by 7 inches. This drum is very similar to a Ludwig Black Beauty or the Pearl "Steve Ferrone" signature model. The Pearl free-floating brass shelled snare is awesome too. And last, but not least, is the Paul Leim signature snare from Yamaha. In any of these models, I like the 14-inch by 6 1/2-inch design.

Drumhead Options

The selecting and tuning of drumheads is as important as what kind of drums you play. I prefer Evans heads in general, but as with drums, I've used many of the other manufacturer's products. Yes, the other companies are making good stuff. But to be honest, I've really enjoyed the tone and consistency of Evans drumheads.

The models are identified by code names. A thin head is a G1, a medium weight is a G Plus, and a thick/double-ply head is called a G2. Evans has even introduced a new design that is slightly heavier than a G1 but is not a double-ply head. It's called a G14. Like the other companies, they are constantly working on new concepts. There are other head designs with muffling strips, holes, and special tone-control designs. I prefer more standard-design heads so that I can choose muffling and tone options by the way I tune and muffle. This is my personal approach, of course. I have used these other special-design heads, so I'll share in general how they affect the tone you can get with them.

Any tone control rings or pin striping will muffle a head. Also, any little pinholes they put in a head will dry it out. Again, this is not my personal preference. I like to be able to make the adjustments myself. Also note that clear heads are brighter sounding than coated heads or any other type of texturing. The coating makes the drum tone a little drier, but you'll probably hear more stick attack because of the textured material. This is a good option to keep in mind if you prefer a drier, muted tone but want to hear more attack. Fiber or other synthetic textured heads have very different tonal effects on a drum, and they are also usually drier or darker sounding than clear or even the regular coated heads. Anyway, it's good to always know your options. The more you experiment, the more you'll learn.

Kick Heads and Tuning

On the kick drum, I use a clear Evans EQ3 on the batter side (that's the side where the mallet strikes). This is a double-ply head, much like the Remo Emperor model. For years I've chosen double-ply heads for the kick batter and the tops of the toms because of their warmth and durability. The front head is usually a medium ply. It's often the head with the company name on it. A 6-inch hole is cut at about the three o'clock position or nine o'clock. I do not like to have a hole in the center of a front bass drum head. Cutting a hole in the middle makes the head lose quite a bit of resonance quickly. Again, I like to be able to make small adjustments. Both heads are tuned so low that they almost sound like a paper bag rattling. You might see them wrinkle as you strike the drum. That's okay, really. If I hear them flopping too much, I will tune them up a little. I'll use a large bath towel or soft pillow for muffling. Make sure the padding touches both front and back heads. Of course you can use more or less padding to adjust the sound of the drum. Don't stuff your kick drum with a huge blanket or stiff foam rubber. That will only choke the shell tone and make your bass drum sound like a cardboard box. Remember: drums must breathe! The shells have to vibrate to create the right tone. I also like to use the curved plastic side of the bass drum beater to get more attack sound from the kick. Keep in mind this is a very modern-radio rock or standard studio approach to tuning.

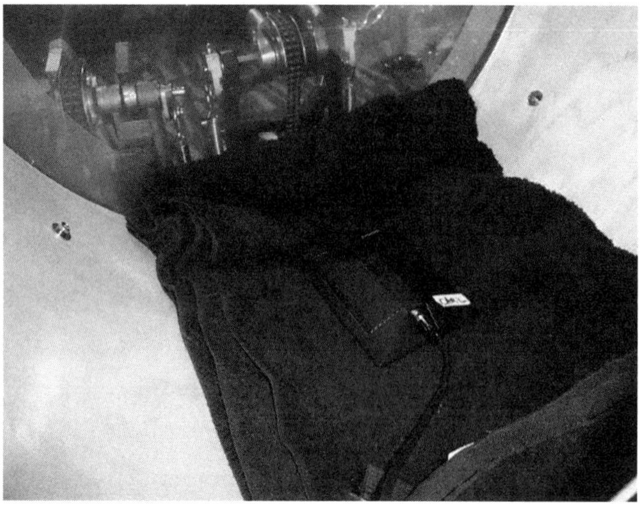

Figure 7.1. Padding inside the kick drum.

When playing jazz, I would definitely choose thinner heads that are coated. This would apply to all the drums. I would also tune in a much higher pitch range, even for the bass drum. There would also be no or very little muffling on any of the drums.

When playing on a song that needs to sound like old-school rock 'n' roll, I would use this same approach of higher tuning with no muffling, but I would probably choose to play larger drums. Sort of like the way John Bonham would play for Led Zeppelin. This is not a typical approach for modern pop songs, and definitely not a standard way of tuning for modern worship music either. But it's still good to know your options.

Tom Heads and Tuning

Tom-toms are the midrange sound of your kit, so you want more of a medium tension on the heads—not floppy like the kick. I also prefer even-sized tom shells. A 10-, 12-, 14-, and 16-inch configuration is my favorite—in standard depths, not power toms. This is a term drum companies use for the deeper or longer tom shells. Clear Evans G2 heads on top and clear G1s or Resonant on the bottom will do the trick. As a reference, these heads are like the Remo Clear Emperor and Clear Ambassador, respectively.

I start with all of the tuning lugs turned just finger tight very evenly around the drum on both top and bottom. If this is all new, try tuning a little at a time until you hear a nice, smooth tone from the drum, not buzzing or floppy sounding. As you increase the tension, you'll notice a point where the drum really rings well. That's a good thing. Take note of the pitch at this lowest range. Hum the sound. If you can, go to a piano or other note-based instrument to find the pitch. Make a note of it. Then you can raise the tension to the tone you like. My tuning approach is to center the resonating tone to a specific pitch rather than letting the ringing tone be a little flat or sharp. Even though an audience doesn't recognize drum pitch like they would piano or guitar, I believe they feel it. This is often why listeners will *feel* they really enjoy the sound of a drum set. They don't know the mechanics of it, but it just feels good. And that's a good thing for sure!

I prefer tuning in intervals of perfect fourths. Sing "Here comes the bride," and with the first two notes, you'll be singing an interval of a fourth. You can also sing a major scale: 1, 2, 3, 4 (do, re, mi, fa), and you'll find it that way. So my normal tuning choices are as follows: the 10-inch tom is a D; the 12-inch, an A; the 14-inch, an E; and the 16-inch is a low B. Try these pitch references as a starting point, but don't hesitate to experiment to find the best tone for your drums. I always suggest going for big pitch intervals when tuning. Avoid tuning any two drums closer than a third apart. By the way, I use this method when tuning all my percussion gear as well. Congas, bongos, timbales, and so forth are always tuned in broad intervals. In recording sessions, I will even tune to the specific keys of the songs, but in most live performance settings, the suggested pitches above work great most of the time. On occasion a certain frequency in a room may force me to tune to different notes to avoid the problem of sympathetic vibration. In other words, a tom or snare won't stop ringing because of its tone responding to that pitch in the auditorium.

If you have odd-size toms, such as a 13-inch drum, try tuning to an F or F♯, or even lower to an E if possible. On a 15-inch drum, a C could sound nice. Try to keep the intervals big so each drum is very distinct. Use very little muffling on your toms, if any. I just roll up a little duct tape, sticky side out, and place it on the head just touching the rim to help control any odd overtones. You could also use some Moon Gel—a very popular drum-muffling product—or even an O-ring. But try adjusting the tuning before muffling the drums.

Figure 7.2. Moon Gel muffling on a tom.

Snare Heads and Tuning

Snare drums should normally be the tight, cracking sound on your kit. Tune them high. Well, most of the time! I use a coated Evans Reverse Power Dot batter head or coated G1 on top and a clear Resonant snare-side head. Yes, there is a difference between a head designed for the top of a snare and the bottom. Bottom snare heads are designed to respond more to the snare wires that need to buzz properly on them. Both heads tuned up pretty tightly should create a high G when played without the snares on. If your snare sounds too dark, it probably won't cut through well. You can tune it up higher if you'd like. Keep tweaking it until you like what you hear. Be sure the snares are adjusted loosely enough to get a good press roll, but tightly enough to get good definition when you play fast notes or ruffs. I'll use a little tissue folded up in a small rectangle about 1 inch by 2 inches attached to the head with some duct tape for muffling. Sometimes I'll use half of an O-ring. It all depends on the drum and the type of music I'm playing. If the style I'm playing needs a bright, popping snare, I might tune a lot tighter and use thinner heads to get as much ringing tone as I can. If the music needs a real fat-sounding snare, I'll use a bigger drum with thick heads and tune it way down. It all depends on the sound I need to create.

I have over a dozen different snares for a variety of sounds I might need for the tour and recording work I do. But normally the big brass snare is my primary choice, and a brass or maple piccolo snare for the second snare that I use to the left of my hi-hat. That drum is tuned really high for a completely different sound from the primary snare.

So there you have it. A superlow kick, midrange toms, and a tight, crackin' snare should create a wide range of drum tones for the music you're making. With good heads and tuning, you can make almost any drum set sound nice.

I know this was a crash course in drum tuning, but you'll get the hang of it. Start here and try other methods, and you'll be amazed at how many different types of sounds you can get out of your drums. Don't be afraid to keep trying until you get the tone you want out of your kit. You'll notice that as your sound gets better, people will enjoy hearing the drums more. Hm, maybe we won't have to play behind Plexiglas anymore—I can dream, can't I? Peace, and happy tuning!

8

Drum Miking for Worship Venues

There are tons of books on drum miking techniques for studio, touring, and clubs, but only a few that really address the challenge of miking a kit for churches. I'm going to add my thoughts and experience to that limited resource, because many drummers and music directors have been asking for some clear information about what works best for miking drums in a typical worship setting. In this chapter, I'll stay focused on what most of you have described as a very frustrating and provoking topic.

First, let's settle the issue in general. *Yes*, drums should be miked in any worship setting. At seminars we do, I almost always hear the comment, "We don't mike our drums at church. Do we need to do that?" Yes, you do. In almost every situation, you should use microphones on the drums. This is for clarity and definition of sound, not to make the drums louder than everyone else. When everyone else is miked or plugged into the PA, if the drums are left out, they will sound muddy and totally unclear in the room, and maybe even on the platform. This is especially true if you are using a drum shield. Some of you have said that you're in "the fish bowl" and don't even mike the drums in that setting. Yikes! Not good.

What About Small Rooms?

Only if you were playing in an extremely small room would I not mike the drum kit. That would be a venue that holds less than 50 people. Even in a situation like this, where we set up very close as a band and the vocal microphones are picking up the kit very well, I still would put a mic in the kick drum. A Shure Beta 52 would be my microphone of choice for any kick drum in any situation. Usually in a small venue, the bass drum will lose definition rather quickly when everyone starts singing, clapping, shouting, and so forth, and a mic in the kick will help keep the low end and pulse of the music more defined.

For what I call the absolute minimum of microphones, I prefer using a kick mic and one overhead mic. It is standard opinion that the overhead should be some kind of condenser mic—not a dynamic mic. Either the Shure SM81 or KSM32 is a great choice for an overhead. You should also use a condenser mic when you are able to separately mike the hi-hat. There are other condenser mics that are less expensive that can do a fine job. Just be sure to stay away from using any dynamic mics for the purpose of capturing the sound of cymbals or the overall drum kit. That is, of course, unless you are doing so to specifically try something sonically different with the drum set.

Using Just Two Microphones

Using just two microphones is a very simple setup. Put the kick mic inside the bass drum using a short mic stand. Do not lay the mic on a pillow, unless it's designed to be used in that way. A mic designed to be used like this would be the Shure Beta 91.

Figure 8.1. Three microphones for the kick drum.

In this picture, the Shure Beta 52 is outside the hole, because there is a Beta 91 inside the kick on the towel. If the 52 were the only mic, I would move it into the drum, directly in the center, pointing toward the kick mallet. I'd then move it according to the sound I want to achieve: closer if I want more attack or "click," farther away if I want to hear more roundness or air. The Yamaha SubKick is used only to add more "superlow" frequencies if desired. I would recommend using it in addition to an internal microphone. The mic inside the bass drum gives you the main source for your kick sound, and then you turn up the SubKick channel to fatten up the tone as much as you'd like. You could use the SubKick as the only source if you want to create the classic Roland 808 electronic kick drum sound. That would definitely be for a specific musical situation. For this discussion, I'll stick with the single-kick mic approach.

A single overhead microphone should be literally positioned "over your head," about a foot or more higher than your head, pointing to the center area looking down at your drum set. I usually stand and look down at the drums and position the mic so it's pointing slightly off-center toward the snare. Make adjustments according to how your engineer thinks he or she is getting the best overall sound of the kit. If you are mixing in stereo, use two overhead mics. But for the minimalist approach, a single mic will do. It's very helpful to have an assistant move this overhead mic around while you play the drums and the engineer works on getting a perfect blended sound.

Figure 8.2. Using two overhead microphones in an A/B configuration.

Overhead mics are the way you get the picture of the whole kit. I start with them and then add individual drum mics for definition. I'm not a trained engineer, but as a drummer, this is how I hear drums first. And this seems to be how the "real" engineers get their drum sound working best.

Using Two Overhead Microphones

If you are using the overhead microphones as the only sound source for the drums, then placement is crucial. Usually when the overheads are only used for cymbals, then they can be pointed more directly at the cymbals and hi-hat. I would prefer using two mics in this situation to get good coverage of only the cymbals. Also, I would use what they call an A/B miking configuration, in which the microphones are placed left and right over the cymbal array. Try to keep equal distance from the snare drum to avoid phasing.

Setting up the overheads in an X/Y pattern gives you a great stereo picture of the kit without the problem of phasing issues. By the way, *phasing* is when a sound source hits two microphones at different times and it cancels the sound out or makes it sound very thin.

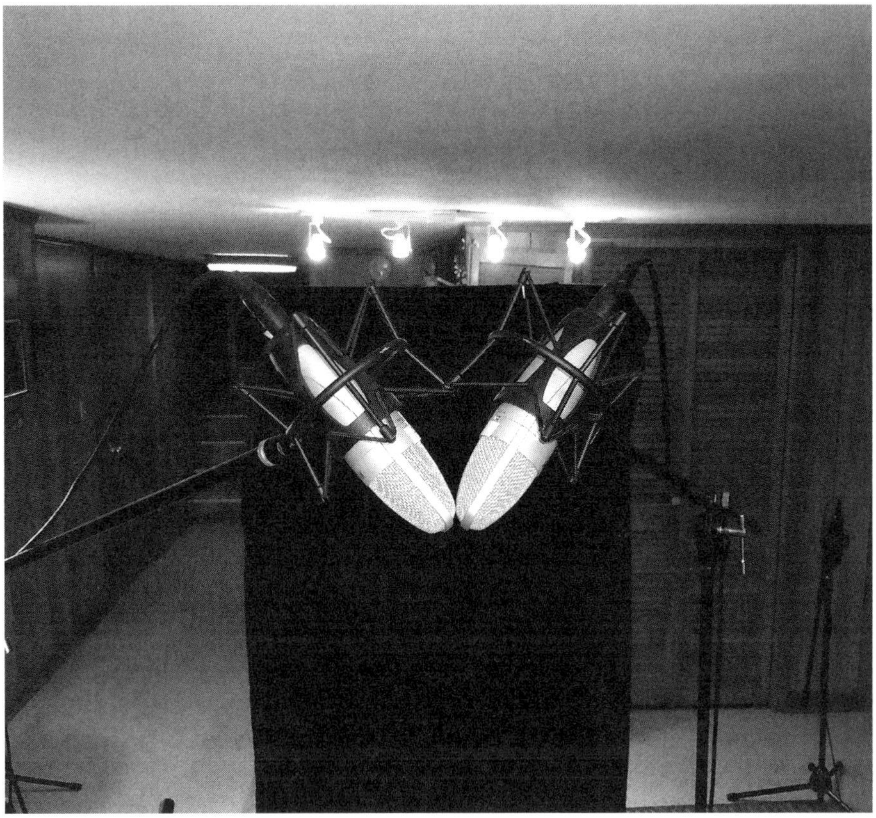

Figure 8.3. Overhead microphones in an X/Y configuration.

Don't get carried away with EQing the kit. Start by moving microphones first and get the best natural sound you can, then EQ as necessary. For drums in general, I would cut those boxy-sounding midrange frequencies around 400 hertz. You'll see this recommendation in many other writings and on many drum-mixing websites. A standard technique is doing a low-frequency cut, which is also called a hi-pass filter, on everything except kick and maybe floor toms. Now let's add the other drums.

Miking the Rest of the Kit

Check out the photos for microphone placement on the hi-hat and snares. These are the angles I start with—about 45 degrees and just over the edge into the drums. I also allow a little breathing room for the drums. The end of the microphones should be 2 to 3 inches off of the head.

Figure 8.4. Miking the snares and hi-hat.

It's great to have an assistant move the mics around as you play, and allow the engineer to stay at the mixing console to listen. You'll be surprised how much the sound changes with very little movement. Keep the back of the mics toward the hi-hat so you get as little hi-hat sound in the snare mics as possible. The hi-hat mic is as far away from the snare drums as possible and about 6 inches high off of the closed hat. I prefer pointing it halfway between the edge and the bell of the top hat.

Tom miking should be approached the same way as the snare drums. A 45-degree angle and about 2 to 3 inches off of the head, just on the edge of the drum.

Figure 8.5. Shure Beta 98s on the toms.

As an exception to the dynamic-mic-on-drums rule, I like to use the Shure Beta 98s on my toms. They are what we call mini-condensers. They have great response to the high-end snap I like to hear from toms, but still reproduce the low tones. These mics don't look like they could do that, but they do! On a budget, I would be happy to use Shure SM57s on all the drums and a PG series of mics for the condensers (Shure PG81). You would save a lot of money without losing that much quality. In fact in many large studios, the SM57 is still a drum standard.

Start with the Basics

Start with a basic miking setup if you're not doing anything at this time. The kick microphone plus an overhead is a great way to launch into drum miking. Remember, you are miking the kit for clarity, not to overpower the rest of the band. And as a drummer, you have to control your dynamics. Adjust to the room you're playing in, whether it's a small chapel, choir room, home meeting or megachurch. Smaller sticks, Hot Rods, or brushes may become necessary tools for your situation. In fact, there are many times when I have to use Hot Rods or brushes and maybe a small stick for side-stick sounds because the acoustics in a particular venue are horrible for drums. It happens to everyone.

Let me know how it works in your situation. You can contact me at my website. I also have a DVD about drum sound on my site called "Drum Miking Made Easy." Check it out if you want to dive in deeper. Blessings on your drum mix.

9

Recording Drums in Worship

Do I approach a recording differently from playing for a live worship or concert event? Absolutely! But before we go any further, let me say that in all things artistic, these are my personal thoughts on the subject as of this day. I'm always trying to learn and stay open to new ideas. Also, another player may feel differently about this, and I would not argue the point. This is just Carl speaking. I do have a lot of experience and training, but I always keep an open mind.

When recording an event, especially in the studio, I feel every element becomes more enhanced. Sort of like the difference between watching a stage play and seeing the movie version of the same story. Things in theater are usually a little more dramatic and over the top. For music I feel it's the same. When you listen to a recording, you are more aware of the smallest details of the musical parts. In a live setting, you become more emotionally affected by the physical and spiritual environment. You don't really zero in on the individual elements of the music or presentation as much.

From the drummer's point of view, this simply means I would probably play more stuff in a purely live event than in a recording situation. In fact, most artists ask for more drum activity in concert settings than when we record. Again, not always, but most of the time, this is the case. Often they want to feel more energy. This translates into more fills or busier grooves than what might have been on the original recording. Maybe even playing the songs at different tempos from the original versions. I guess this means that I do what I'm asked to do. Hm! Imagine that! Remember, it's always about serving people. But if they want me to copy the record and play it like it was written, I can still do that.

The Recording Microscope

When recording, we get down to the nitty-gritty of the music, analyzing every detail. I definitely think in terms of leaving a lot of space for all the elements of the arrangement. Vocals and melodic instruments alike get my attention. I never think of drums and percussion as being separated from the rest of the music. I purposely try to leave room for riffs or melodic lines from all of the instruments involved. This often means I won't play a fill or groove that takes up too much room sonically.

In a live setting, I'm still aware of all of the musical elements, but I might take more liberty in enhancing all of the other parts. This could mean playing more cymbal and hi-hat parts over an intro, doing more fills to lead into verses and choruses, or even making the basic groove itself more complex to give the music greater momentum. It's a fine line between enhancing the music and getting too busy. I try to remember to ask the leader how it's feeling for him or her. Is he or she happy with my approach? I want to know. So don't be afraid to communicate with your team—especially those in charge.

When recording, I'll think of how the drums sound on tape more than how they sound for the room. I go to the control room and listen to the rehearsal recordings to see if the drums are tracking well. What sounds great in the auditorium may not be what is getting to the recorded tracks. So my focus is on what the end result is going to be. Yes, you should record the rehearsals. In the world of producing records, the motto is "The red light is always on." This gives you the opportunity to check things out before you are doing the actual live event. Plus, it gives the producer several options in the recording of a song. If something happens to an individual track, or even an entire take during the live event, you are able to copy a previous track from a rehearsal take that was done well and "fly it in." Which is just recording slang for copying into the final performance take. This works best if you are playing to a click track. And today that has become the norm for recording, even in a live situation.

I'll listen carefully to every element. Is every drum channel being heard? Do the toms all match in terms of sustain and character of sound? Is there a good balance between the left and right overhead microphones? There are times you have to move the mics a bit to get the right sound. Often I'll need to change heads if they are sounding a little dull. As a rule,

I do not change heads on the day of a live recording. I have found they are still stretching during that day, and by the middle of a long set of songs, I need to tune them again but can't stop in the middle of an event. In the studio it's okay to change heads more, because I can tune up before every take. So my rule is to change heads the morning before the evening recording and let the new heads settle in during a final rehearsal or run-through. Then I'll check the tuning again before they let the audience into the room.

To Muffle or Not to Muffle

In a live performance, I might muffle the drums more to control the overtones in the auditorium. For studio sessions, we would use more "noise gates" and compression for that during the mixdown of the record. Engineers have told me my sound is a little too open and resonant for them to mix well in certain rooms. I always try to make it work for them and trust their perspective. But if we're recording, I'll ask them to gate the drums a little if they have the equipment. It can be a little tricky to make a live recording sound really great. I just personally like the drums to ring a lot. In the end, it's always about serving the vision of the artist and producer. Always be willing to take instruction, and do your best to help them feel they've found the right sound for their music.

Sometimes I'll tune tighter in a live setting to cut through a large room or a dull-sounding auditorium. It seems the higher pitches can cut through better than the lower tones. I don't always do this, but I will sometimes experiment more with changing my sound and style when I can risk it not working so well. Nonrecorded events are great for this. Sound checks and rehearsals are also great for exploring your creativity, but once I am in a recording situation, I'll settle into an idea that makes everyone happy. I will never change ideas and experiment once we've locked into an arrangement. What a drummer plays affects the whole band.

As I've said before, it's a good idea to record everything you do. Even if you're the only one who listens, it's a great tool for checking out how you really sound. Plus, when it comes time to work on a real recording, you will have already been preparing your ears for how the drums sound from that perspective. The sonic quality of a drum kit in the open air is very different from what you will hear from a recording. It's quite an eye opener—or should I say ear opener. So make this part of your regular activity as a performer.

If your drums are set up in a Plexiglas cage, it would be a good idea to open up the booth a little bit when it's time to record. If the shield is too close to the drums, they will sound harsh. In a nonrecorded situation, this is not a major problem. But when you hear the playback, the drums will sound brittle, as if you are in a small box. Which is exactly where you are when using a booth or cage. Move the glass away just a little, and it will help. I try to leave enough space to walk around the kit. This allows the drums and cymbals to breathe. Plus, you're able to walk around the drums more easily if you have to move microphones or cables. Also, put foam acoustic panels along the bottom 3 feet of the inside of the booth. This will help in reducing the brittle tone that Plexiglas creates. It would also be a good idea *not* to set up in a corner or along the back wall. The reflecting sound from those positions is horrible. Remember: drums need room to breathe, just like people.

Microphone Choices for Recording

I do let the engineer and producer choose microphones and their placement. But if they ask me, I always ask for Shure mics. Again, that's a personal choice. My live recording mic configuration is not much different from what I would choose for any live event. I may choose to use fewer mics if we are not recording, as I have described in a previous chapter.

I'll use two mics for the kick drum. A Shure Beta 91 inside the drum on the muffling towel right in the middle, and a Beta 52 on the outside of the drum about a couple of inches outside the hole. If there are enough channels, I will also add a Yamaha SubKick to pick up the superlow tones of the kick. This does mean three separate channels for the bass drum. Shure SM57s for all the snare drums is a must: set at a 45 degree angle just at the edge of the snare, pointing toward the center of the drum. Shure Beta 98s on the toms work great, but many engineers prefer a large-diaphragm dynamic microphone, such as a Sennheiser 421. I will leave about a three-finger gap—a couple of inches—between the capsule and the tom head. Shure KSM32s for the overheads are always a great choice. Please observe the "3 to 1 rule" to avoid phasing: the mics should be at least 3 feet away from each other for every 1 foot of distance from your recording subject. In this case, we're talking about cymbals. Last, but not least, I use a Shure KSM137 for the hi-hat: about 6 inches high off the top of the hi-hats on the opposite side of the snare drum. You want as much distance or separation from the snare as you can get.

Figure 9.1. Overhead microphone placement.

Figure 9.2. Overhead microphones, side view.

A Clean Drum Sound

Another tip for preparing to record is to be sure your drums only make drum sounds. Keep cymbal stands quiet with proper nylon sleeves and felt washers in place on the stems of the holders. You don't want to hear hardware rattling or buzzing during your recording. Also, keep your kick and hi-hat pedals lubricated and adjusted properly so you don't hear any squeaking or grinding noises. Be mindful of drums or hardware bumping into each other. Keep clear gaps between all the pieces. You may even have to put a small foam or cloth padding on drums that are close to other pieces, so you don't hear them if they start to shake too much. This does happen in the middle of many exciting musical moments. Things just start moving around.

Be sure to set up on a nice rug or solid piece of carpeting so you don't hear floor noises. Also, watch for microphones and stands moving and rubbing against the drums. You may not notice it at the moment, but you will hear the bumping sound or vibration when you listen to the playback, which might ruin a perfectly good take, or at least force you to mute that mic during the mix. Bummer! Maybe not a bad thing for the mic on tom No. 8, but it would be terrible for the snare mic. Also, for me, I don't like to clamp mics onto my drums or stands. The vibrations may not be very noticeable for live events, but again, you can hear the difference on a recording.

Better Drum and Cymbal Separation

You may also have to raise the height of your cymbals a bit if they are too close to your drums. This can really help with the separation of the drum sounds from the cymbals. Come on, be a good sport and try it. You'll love the sound you get from the drums and cymbals by giving them a little more space. It really does not have to be that drastic of a change to make a difference. I've known some drummers to really fight with engineers about their setup. Try to be flexible. As long as it doesn't destroy your ability to play, try to accommodate the people trying to make you sound great.

The Click Again

Be sure to practice and perform with a click track as much as possible. Get your groove locked down so you sound good when it comes time to do that recording. This would be a great idea for the whole team, but for sure it is a must for every drummer.

Keep refining all of your drumming skills so that you can fully enjoy the gift the Lord has given you. There are things you can do differently when it comes to recording your drum performances, but ultimately you want everything you do to sound great. After all, the red light is always on!

10

Worship Drummer Warm-ups

People often ask me how I prepare for an event. They want to know if there is a difference in the way a drummer should get ready for sessions, concerts, or worship services. The simple answer I give is that I approach every job the same way. In other words, there is the big picture, or foundational principles that apply to everything in life, but there are slight variations in the details. So let's dive in!

The thing that remains the same for me is that I approach every situation as a technical and a spiritual task. There are mechanical details involved in anything you do, and then there's the spiritual aspect of what the Lord has called you to do in each situation. So simply speaking, be prepared mentally, physically, and spiritually. This perspective on not just music, but life in general, keeps your world functioning properly.

The Details of Events

I first consider the type of event I have to prepare for. If it's a seminar event, I make sure I know the classes I'm teaching and that my notes are ready. Quite often my drum clinic will be in a different room than the concert hall or sanctuary. In that case, I check with the staff to be sure the right drum kit is available. I also need a small PA system with a microphone and inputs for my click device and tracks I send from the output of my laptop. I know seminars are different than other performance settings, but I thought I'd throw that in as a bonus. You're welcome!

Prepare the Music

The biggest job for me in every situation is music preparation. That's usually the first item on my checklist. For sessions, they usually don't send out music ahead of time. The producer or artist will just show the band the tunes when we come to the session. But I will always ask if there are demos of the songs or if there are certain reference recordings I should listen to. That way I can get an idea of the style and vibe of the music we'll be working on. I'll also ask what drum sounds they want for the project and make sure I bring the right equipment to the job. That could mean I have to buy something, but usually I have enough drum gear to cover the call. Hearing the demos early helps me think more deeply about the music and allows for some creative thinking before the session. I often hear drum sounds or grooves, or even percussion and drum loop ideas, when I have a chance to live with the songs for a while. I always feel a little more ahead of the game when this happens.

For live events, if I'm working with artists I've already played for, there's not much music preparation involved unless they ask for new songs to be added to the list. Even if you work with someone a lot, it's a good idea to touch base and see if there's anything new that they are thinking about. It does happen.

I try to be very proactive in my work. I'll make the call and chat with Paul Baloche or Don Moen or other artists I've worked with to see if they want to try out new songs they're writing or even if they are going to cover another artist's material. I just try to stay in touch. If there's no time to get the CDs, I just download songs from the Internet or ask them to send MP3s if possible.

When I'm working with new artists, I definitely work hard on their material. I'll ask for a current song list they're using, what projects I need to listen to, and whatever charts or lead sheets they have available. Right now, in fact, I'm preparing to play for the Integrity Seminars4Worship, and I'm learning material for about six artists at each event. Sheeesh! I'm tired already. Today I'm downloading files and charts so I can rehearse their songs. So rule No. 1 is: *Get the music ready!*

Check Your Gear

Rule No. 2 is gear preparation. Do I have all the drums and percussion instruments I need to play everything I'm hearing in the music? What about electronics, samples, loops, and so forth? I try to have all the bases covered. Even if I have all the equipment and software, it's very important to know that it's in good working order. There's nothing more frustrating than going into a job and finding that something doesn't work right. Besides electronics and software, I'm also checking mechanical parts, such as kick pedals, hi-hats, and hardware, for wear and tear. Also inspect drumheads and your stick bag to make sure you have doubles of everything you might need for a job. Even at church events or other small jobs you might think of as normal or unimportant, I always have double stuff. In reality, every job is important and deserves our best efforts. I always have a spare kick pedal and snare drum handy, as well as a spare-parts bag. In that bag will be a hi-hat clutch, springs, screws, snare straps, washers, cymbal sleeves, duct tape, and so forth. As much as possible, I plan and prepare for problems that may occur. If and when they do, I'm ready! My motto is, "Have two of everything if at all possible."

When traveling, many times I'm playing rented equipment or brand-new gear right out of the box. Either way I always go to the venue ahead of the rest of the team to be sure everything is in good working order. There have been moments when critical pieces were missing, and being early allowed me time to call for help and get whatever was needed.

All of this applies to my electronic gear too. I have samplers, drum machines, laptops, and metronomes that need to be checked. If the tour is able to provide it, I might ask for a second setup of electronics, to be sure I can cover the job if something blows up. In most current situations, everyone is taking care of their electronic music needs with laptops. This includes sound modules, sampling, looping, sequencing, effects, and supplemental tracks. The cool thing about it is that several players in the band can duplicate systems in each laptop. We will even carry extra hard drives to back up any critical information. In case of an emergency, you can always ask another player to use his or her rig. Of course if you have the budget, the best thing to do is to double up on your own gear. Yes, that means having a second laptop. This may be needed if everyone is using his or her computer for the gig. Then borrowing one is out of the question. So again, rule No. 2: *Check, and double-check all your gear. And have duplicates if you can.*

The Final Preparations

When it comes time for being "on the job," the first two rules should have already been observed. Once you're there, you and your gear have to be ready. I can then take care of the final preparations before playing. That includes some physical warm-up time and some soul searching.

After all this time, I still like to do 10 to 20 minutes of rudimental exercises before I play. Combinations of singles, doubles, paradiddles, and flams help me to loosen up very nicely. I try to incorporate my feet as well. Just play a basic four on the floor with the kick foot, and two and four with the hi-hat foot. Then play your hand exercises over that. If possible have a metronome plugged into your ear while you do this, and play to the click. Of course you can do variations of those ideas or come up with your own routine. The main thing is to feel warmed up and physically loose before you have to play the job. Any kind of tension or tightness will cause you to be less responsive.

Even do a few physical stretches from any workout routine. Just like when I get ready to jog, I'll do some leg and arm stretches, light twists, squats, pushups, and so forth. So that's rule No. 3: *Pre-gig drum warm-ups.*

Here are a few simple sticking patterns to get you started. Play them on a soft practice pad if you can, or even a chair cushion if you have to. You can do variations of these as you choose, and also do them starting with the left hand instead of the right. Count along out loud if this is new to you: "1-e-&-ah, 2-e-&-ah, 3-e-&-ah, 4-e-&-ah."

R	L	R	L	R	L	R	L	R	L	R	L	R	L	R	L
R	R	L	L	R	R	L	L	R	R	L	L	R	R	L	L
R	L	R	R	L	R	L	L	R	L	R	R	L	R	L	L
R	R	L	R	L	L	R	L	R	R	L	R	L	L	R	L
R	R	R	L	R	R	R	L	R	R	R	L	R	R	R	L

Figure 10.1. Basic sticking pattern warm-ups, plus feet.

Besides playing a duple feel, it's also important to play patterns in a triplet feel. Use these patterns counting "1-trip-let, 2-trip-let," and so on. Or I prefer counting "1-la-lee, 2-la-lee." I think these syllables fall off the tongue easier. You can choose to count either way. It's also a good idea to count out loud at first and then gradually allow the counting to become internalized as you become more comfortable.

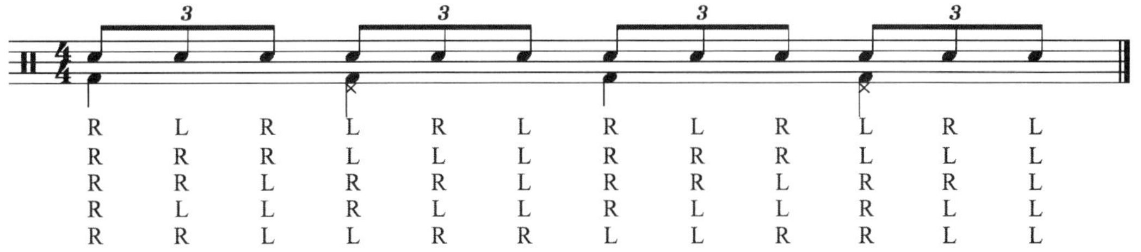

Figure 10.2. Triplet sticking patterns with basic foot pattern.

Spiritual Readiness

Finally, do a spiritual warm-up. Prayer, reading the Word, or just being still before the Lord are all great ways to prepare to minister to the Lord in worship and to the lead people. Do not take the stage without having your heart focused on the Lord and the ministry aspect of your music. Even if your time is really short, do what you can. I feel it's important to have some time alone for this, but I like to have time with the band and ministry team as well. In most settings, I try to allow 30 minutes of group time to fellowship, settle our thoughts, and have time to pray together before we go to the platform to lead worship together. Don't think of this as an empty ritual. Really press into this routine, and make it a "holy habit." If you sense that your group prayer times are becoming mundane, shake things up by asking others to pray or read. It would even be great to have one of your pastors or intercessory prayer team come in and pray with you. Mix it up. So last, but not least, rule No. 4: *A spiritual warm-up is a must before you play.*

There you have it. I hope this helps you in your journey of being a fully prepared worship drummer.

11

Drum Grooves for Worship

I just finished analyzing the Top 100 worship songs on the CCLI list. CCLI stands for Christian Copyright Licensing International: an organization to help churches and ministry groups stay legal with song and video licensing. Their website always keeps a current list of popular worship songs being used around the world. It's a valuable tool in tracking and learning about modern music in the church.

As a drummer, I was looking for all the different grooves that a player would have to learn to be able to perform all of these songs. Because so many worship leaders and drummers have asked about a simple approach to learning what it would take to start playing in a worship band, I thought I'd start with this list, and see if I could come up with a system that would work. To my amazement, there were only seven basic grooves that a drummer needed to learn to play on a worship team. No, not thirty, twenty, or even ten. There are just seven grooves! I was amazed. Now, that doesn't mean that it's simple to become a great drummer, but at least there are some easy workable patterns that will get you started.

You must realize there are many variations to the seven grooves, but the basics will still apply. Once you've learned seven fundamental drum ideas, you are on your way to playing hundreds of songs. What gets tricky is learning song structures, specific patterns, drum fills, dynamics, various tempos, and so on. But the main feel for all of these still can be broken down into seven major groups. Consequently I decided to release a new DVD in which I explain and demonstrate the seven grooves for worship along with a few variations and practice concepts to help. Of course there is a big emphasis on practicing with—you guessed it—a metronome! There are also a few examples of playing with drum loops, because that is such a major part of what drummers have to be able to do in contemporary worship.

Seeing something demonstrated in order to learn it is absolutely worth a thousand words of explanation. So if you are interested in seeing what I've come up with, you can get the DVD at my website. There's also a special drummers' package of all of my drum DVDs, plus two extras where I also teach with Paul Baloche and team at Paul's website: www.leadworship.com. On my site, there is also a free download of my CCLI list analysis, so you can see all of the songs that fit into the seven categories. Finally, there are excerpts from my DVD series in the DVD-ROM that comes with this book.

Of course as a sidenote, there are thousands of great drum video concepts available all over the web. Just check out your favorite drummers on YouTube or drummerworld.com or any of the other great drum sites.

Okay, enough about the DVDs and websites. Now onto the seven grooves!

1. Straight eighth-note rock and pop grooves.
2. Eighth-note with sixteenth-note fillers—the alternative rock groove.
3. The sixteenth-note train groove—for rock or Latin styles.
4. Eighth- and sixteenth-note feels used in ballads—the slow songs.
5. 6/8 feel, felt in two—the majestic feel.
6. Shuffle or swing feel—a triplet minus the middle (1 _ 3, 1 _ 3).
7. Odd time signatures—3/4, 5/4, and so on.

Groove No. 1: The Eighth-Notes

The first drum groove is probably the easiest for everyone. Rock drumming 101 for sure. Play straight eighth-notes with your right hand, or your left if you prefer, on the hi-hat or ride cymbal. Counting "1 & 2 & 3 & 4 &." Then playing, count 1 on the kick drum, 2 on the snare, 3 on the kick, and then 4 on the snare. Using variations of this idea covers a lot of songs. Some examples from the CCLI list include "Blessed Be the Name," "Forever," "Beautiful One," "Everlasting God" and over 20 more. Again, on the DVD you can see everything, but even just starting with this basic counting exercise and then playing along with the tunes is great foundational practice. Here are a few eighth-note grooves to get you started.

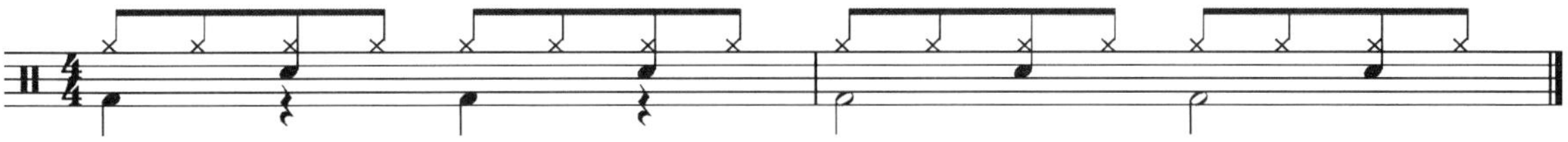

Figure 11.1. Basic eighth-note groove with half-note kick drum.

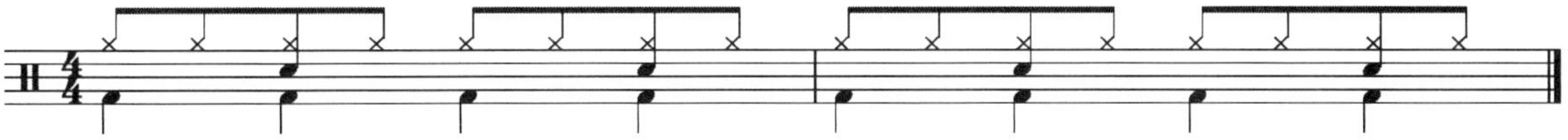

Figure 11.2. Basic eighth-note groove with quarter-note kick drum.

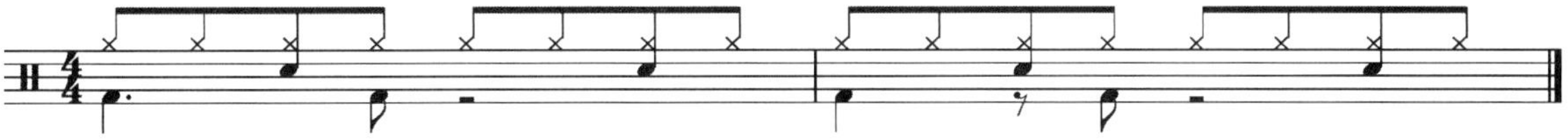

Figure 11.3. Basic eighth-note groove with dotted-eighth kick drum

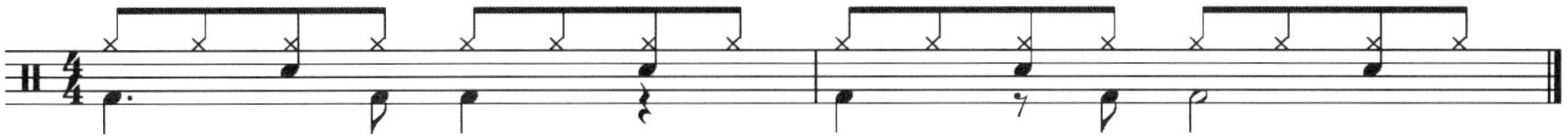

Figure 11.4. Basic eighth-note groove with "& 3" kick pattern.

Groove No. 2: Eighth-Notes with Sixteenth-Note Fillers

Groove No. 2 builds on the basics of No. 1, but starts to incorporate sixteenth-notes being played in between the eighth-notes of the lead hand. Even though we count eighth-notes, we want to feel the sixteenth-notes. So I start counting the in-between notes as well. In the first exercise of this pattern, we play "1-e-&, 2-&, 3-e-&, 4-&," but I feel the constant subdivision of sixteenth-notes in my head—counting or feeling internally, "1e&ah 2e&ah 3e&ah 4e&ah." Be sure the in-between notes are perfectly steady. We call the softer, filler notes "ghost notes," because they're quieter than the others. Their presence is felt more than heard, like a ghost. *Boo!* (Sorry, corny joke!)

Anyway, try this basic exercise to get the feel of it. If needed, play only the hand pattern first. Then add the kick drum later. Also, remember to go slower at first. Speed up according to how smoothly you play. Accuracy is more important than speed.

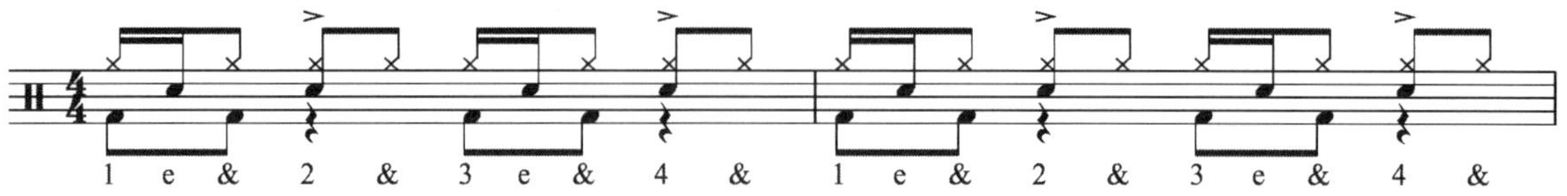

Figure 11.5. Basic "1-e-&" hand pattern with eighth-note kick drum.

Now let's add an extra sixteenth-note to the hands. You can leave out the kick-drum note at first, but then feel free to add kick notes on any count you like. Start with whatever feels easy, and then add the kick as your coordination feels better.

Figure 11.6. Hand exercise with "&-ah-3-e-&" pattern.

In this kind of groove, the kick pattern also starts to fall on various parts of the sixteenth-note line. The next figure shows one of the most popular kick patterns in modern worship. Some songs that fit this groove from the list are "How Great Is Our God," "Here I Am to Worship," "God of Wonders," and many more. Here's the groove without any snare ghost notes, just a strong backbeat.

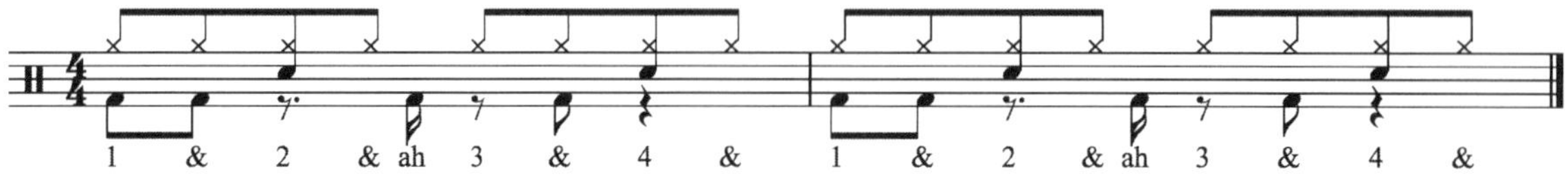

Figure 11.7. Basic eighth groove with kick filler, or syncopation as it's officially known.

Now let's try adding the ghost-note fillers on the snare drum. If doing all of them feels awkward, try adding just one part of them at a time, such as only doing the "1-e-&" pattern first. Then you can step-by-step at the other ghost notes as you have better control of the pattern. You will also notice that bar 2 of this exercise looks different than bar 1, but they are exactly the same pattern. I wanted you to see them scored differently so you would be comfortable seeing the groove in both styles.

Figure 11.8. Snare ghost notes added to basic kick pattern.

Groove No. 3: Sixteenth-Note Patterns

The third groove is also based on counting sixteenth-notes. In this case, you should play all the sixteenths on the hi-hat and then use your lead hand, which for most players is the right hand to hit backbeats on the snare. The backbeat is almost always the 2 and 4 counts of a measure of music. This basic feel would be called a "train beat" in drummers' slang. Kick patterns can vary from all quarter-notes being played to just downbeats, which are the 1 and 3 counts. Once those basic kick patterns are comfortable, then you can work on playing patterns that use any count in the measure. Start with this basic version, and then add kick-drum notes as you feel comfortable.

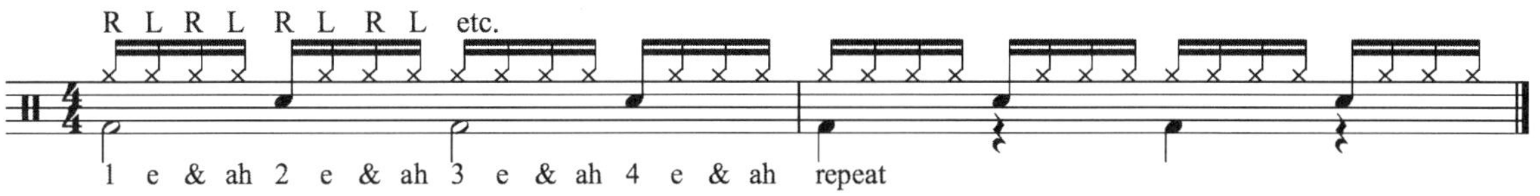

Figure 11.9. Basic sixteenth-note train groove.

If you feel unsteady playing the constant sixteenth-notes, go back to this foundational exercise. Start by practicing a single-stroke roll on a practice pad. Set the metronome at a medium to slow tempo—about 70 bpm (beats per minute) is a good starting tempo—and play it for at least 4 to 5 minutes without stopping. Playing a RLRL RLRL pattern (the single-stroke roll) constantly without a break will help build up the concentration and control to keep this feel going. Then you can gradually build your speed over time, eventually reaching speeds of over 100 bpm and faster. But be aware that being fast is not the goal. Learning to play precisely and smoothly is the first priority. Make sure both hands look and sound exactly the same. Of course, this would be the case if you use matched grip. Traditional grip will look different, but it should still sound the same from left to right stroke. The return height of the stroke should match in both hands no matter what grip you use. Then work on speeding things up gradually. Here are some songs from the list you must learn: "Open the Eyes of My Heart," "Forever," "Come, Now Is the Time to Worship," and "Trading My Sorrows."

In the next figure is a very popular kick drum pattern that is used in many of these songs. Once you feel solid playing the kick on half-notes, quarter-notes, and some eighth-note patterns, try doing this one. It adds the "ah" of 1 and the "&" of 2 to the basic groove. Be aware of how the "ah" count must line up to your left hand—if you're leading with the right, of course. Go slower if there is any *flamming* of the notes. This is a term we use to describe notes that do not line up perfectly against the lead hand. Listen carefully as you play.

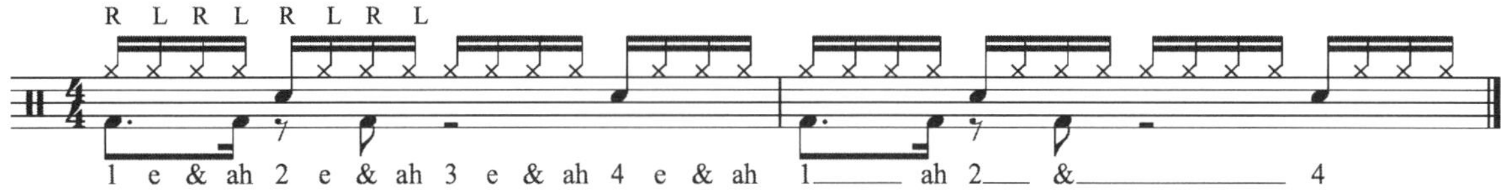

Figure 11.10. The dotted-eighth, sixteenth, and "&" of 2 kick-pattern.

Here's just a simple addition of another kick note to the pattern. It's the "&" of 3. Always by using your hand pattern as a guide, you can try adding any kick note to the groove as you like. Remember to slow down as needed to get the parts to line up perfectly. Then gradually increase your tempo little by little.

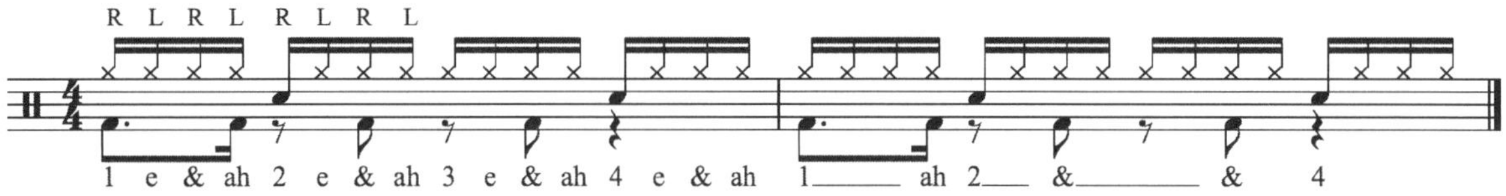

Figure 11.11. Adding the "&" of the 3 count to the kick pattern.

Groove No. 4: The Slow Sixteenth-Note Songs

Playing ballads or slow songs was marked as a separate groove group because drummers often struggle playing at slower tempos. Even though technically the counting and patterns are just like what we've already learned, the mental and emotional way to make a ballad work is different. Primarily I work on counting and feeling more notes than I'm actually playing. This is a key to playing slow songs with excellence. So even though I might actually play eighth-notes as the ride pattern, I will always be counting sixteenth-notes or feeling that kind of rhythm in my head while I play.

A very helpful tool in playing ballads is to set your metronome to click double-time. In other words, if the tempo is set at 60 bpm, have your metronome set at 120 bpm, or have it subdivide the quarter-note into eighths and sixteenths if it has that option. Try playing these popular slow songs from the CCLI favorites list: "Breathe," "Above All," and "As the Deer."

As a beginning exercise, go ahead and play all of the sixteenth-notes on your ride hand (lead hand). Then you can later start accenting the eighth-note part of the ride, and then eventually try the pattern only playing basic eighth-notes with your lead hand.

Here's the most popular version of this groove. You can leave out some of the kick drum notes at first if you feel they don't line up. Slow down and count out loud as you build this groove up. It's okay to take patterns a piece at a time until they feel natural.

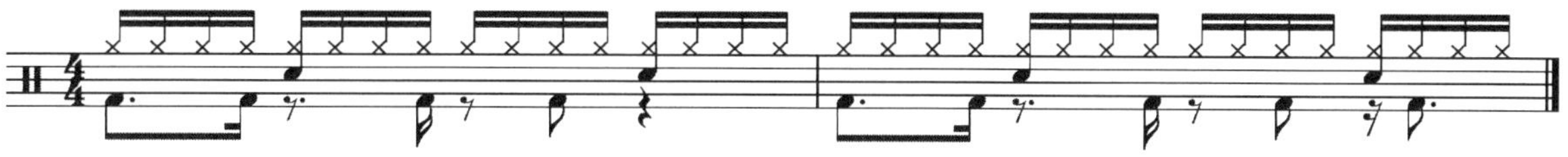

Figure 11.12. A slow ballad groove with a sixteenth-note ride.

Here's the pattern accenting the eighth-notes more in the lead hand. I've also changed the kick pattern a little to simplify it as you get the feel. But start adding more notes as you have good control of the groove.

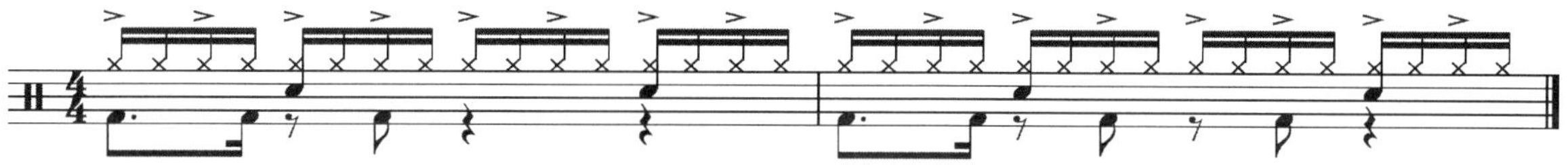

Figure 11.13. Accenting eighth-notes on the ride pattern.

You can always play this feel with only an eighth-note ride pattern, but it always seems to help maintain the momentum of the groove if you at least play lightly on the other sixteenth-notes. Remember that all of these grooves are really just the foundations for all of these concepts. You should always listen to the original recordings and copy what you hear as closely as possible.

Groove No. 5: The 6/8 Majestic Feel

Groove No. 5 is the classic 6/8 feel. I call it the majestic feel. For songs like "He Is Exalted," "Indescribable," and "Famous One," it works perfectly played almost the same way in each case. Although I'm always trying to come up with clever variations for any idea, sometimes the best way is the simplest.

All six notes of the count are played with your lead hand: "1 2 3 4 5 6." Then you place kick and snare hits on the 1 and 4 count respectively. We often say this groove is felt "in 2" because we split the 6/8 measure (or bar) into two pieces. The kick drum hits the downbeat (1) and the snare hits the backbeat (4, in this case). So the feel you end up with is counting three notes for each downbeat and backbeat. Here's the basic pattern.

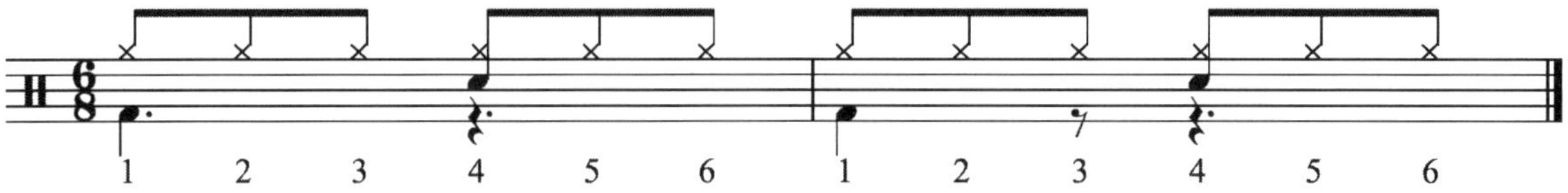

Figure 11.14. The 6/8 majestic feel.

Here's the pattern adding the usual kick drum pick-up note into the 4 count on the snare. You hear this pattern on many songs, such as Chris Tomlin's "Indescribable."

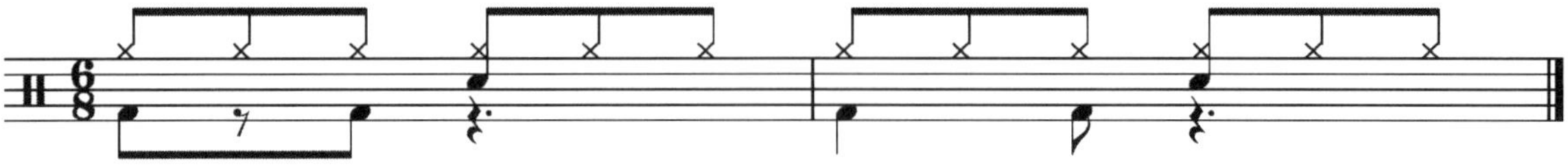

Figure 11.15. Added kick notes to the 6/8 feel.

As you become more comfortable with this groove, try adding "ghost notes" in between your lead hand to create a little more momentum in a song. Again, be sure to be accurate even with the softer notes. Count smoothly "1 & 2 & 3 & 4 & 5 & 6 &" as you play. The feel depends on it. The kick pattern can even be played in between the lead hand according to the song you're playing.

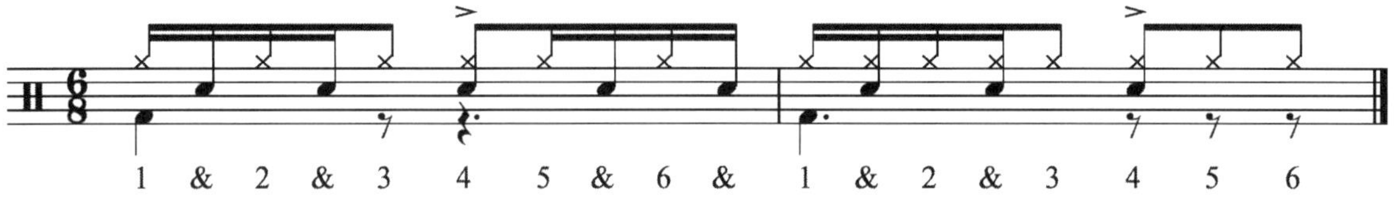

Figure 11.16. Adding ghost notes to the 6/8 feel.

Figure 11.17. Ghost notes and extra kick notes added to the 6/8.

Groove No. 6: The Shuffle and Swing Feel

Groove No. 6 only had one example in the CCLI Top 100 list, but there are other songs beyond that. A shuffle or swing feel was only found in the song "Victory in Jesus," an old classic. In popular or jazz music, we hear this type of feel all the time. But sacred music in general does not make use of it very much. The few songs I found in gospel music that swing or use a triplet subdivision were not even on the CCLI top songs list. Let's look at this rare gospel feel.

To play a shuffle properly, count or feel the triplet on every beat. "1-trip-let, 2-trip-let, 3-trip-let, 4-trip-let" is one way to count it. Let's first play it using all the triplets.

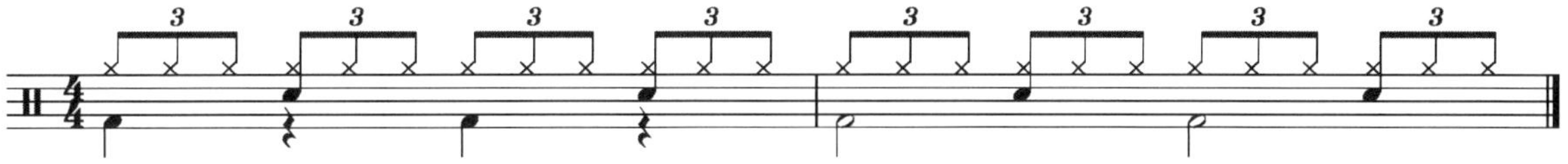

Figure 11.18. Basic triplet groove.

You could just say "tri-pa-let, tri-pa-let" over and over, but I think that becomes rather tedious when you're trying to play along. I've heard some players count it like this: "1-la-lee, 2-la-lee, 3-la-lee, 4-la-lee." Any of these will work.

The only thing with a shuffle is that you don't play the middle note. So even though you're feeling the triplet, you only play the first and third note of the group: "1_ 3,1_ 3,1_ 3,1_ 3" and so on. Now try a simple shuffle groove. You should feel like your lead hand is always pumping or coming down on the 1. Start slow, and go for the feel of it first. On this groove, I did write the ride pattern in the second bar with different notes, but it's still the same count. Again, I do this so you get used to seeing patterns written in different ways.

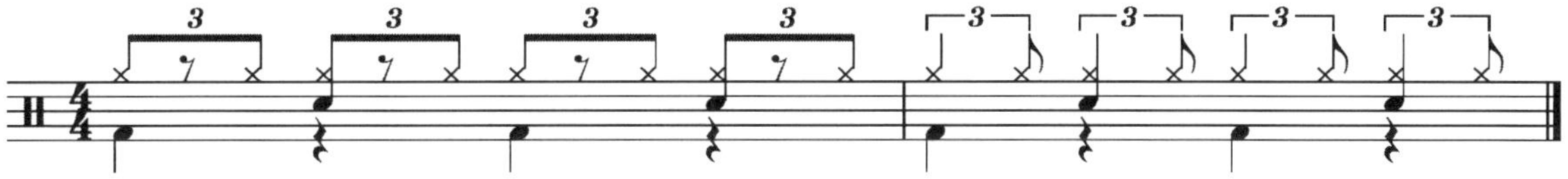

Figure 11.19. The basic shuffle groove.

As with the other patterns, you should always try adding kick drum notes to it as you become more comfortable with the basics. Always use your lead hand as a guide, and add to its count or between it.

The next step in building your shuffle groove is to play it in a half-time feel. This is when we feel the kick and snare pattern on the half-notes and not on the quarter-notes. Here's the basic approach to this feel.

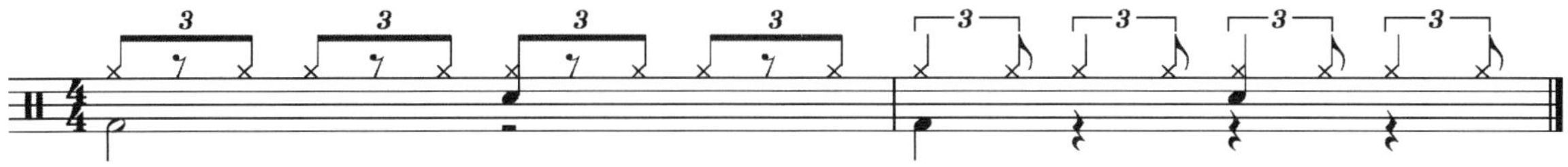

Figure 11.20. The half-time shuffle.

Now let's add some extra kick-drum notes to this groove.

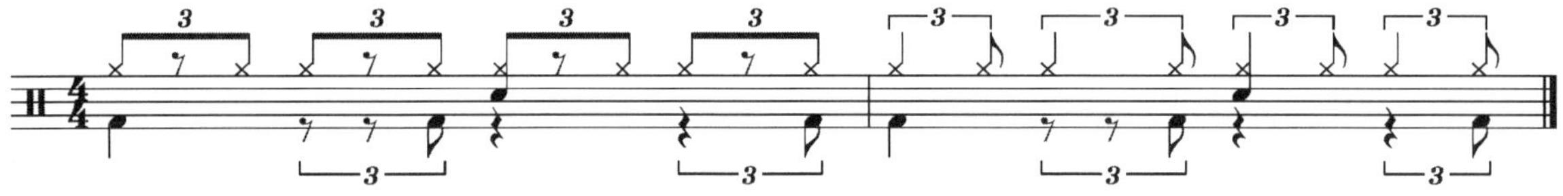

Figure 11.21. The half-time shuffle with extra kick notes.

I used this feel with variations on the kick drum on the song "Arms Open Wide" from the Paul Baloche project *Offering*. Other tunes that work are Ron Kenoly's "The King of Kings Is Coming" from his *Majesty* project. Paul Wilbur's song "Holy Fire" is a fast shuffle "in four." At first, this feel is really tricky. Like all other patterns, start slow and build at your own pace. You'll get it.

Adding ghost notes to the shuffle feel is a very common thing to do. The best way to get use to this is to play the hand parts first. The lead hand plays the regular shuffle pattern, and your other hand will fill in all the middle notes softly on the snare drum. Try it slowly at first, and then speed up as you gain control of the pattern.

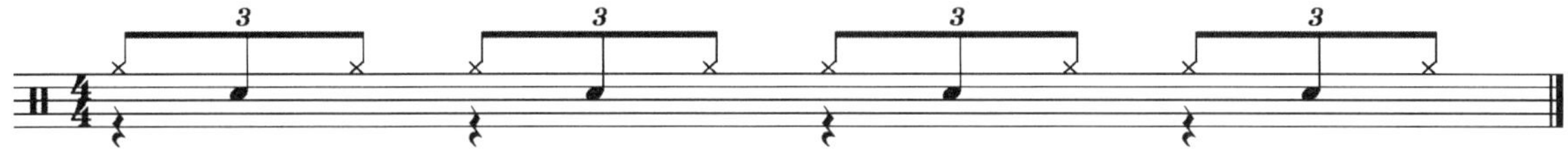

Figure 11.22. Shuffle ghost-note exercise.

Once this feels relaxed and like second nature to you, you can add it in to the groove. Add just one ghost note at a time if you like, and make each one feel perfect. Getting in the ghost note after the accented backbeat will be the trickiest one. It feels like you just let the stick bounce a little after you smack the 2 and 4, but you still must control it so it doesn't hit at random. Always keep your fingers in touch with the stick, but don't grip it too tightly. When you add them all in, it will look like this.

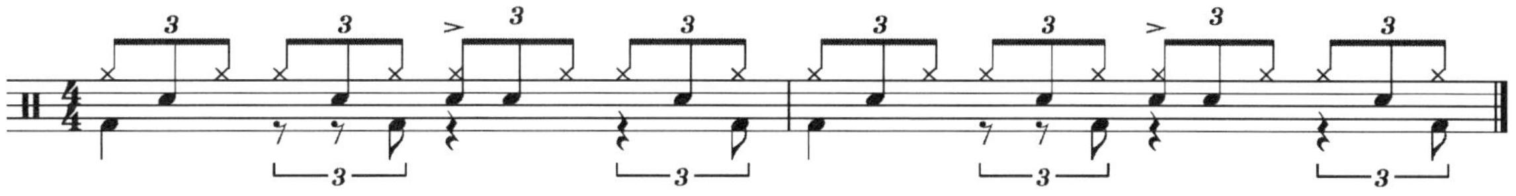

Figure 11.23. Half-time shuffle groove with all ghost notes.

Groove No. 7: Odd Time Signatures

The last groove idea is playing in odd time signatures. The list only contained typical odd meters such as 3/4 and 5/4 time signatures, although other music can expand into many other options. The subdivision of the beat, such as eighths, sixteenths, and triplets, can be used in any of these meters, but most of the record examples they offered on CCLI were straight time-feels (nontriplets). Making this a separate group was based upon the challenges of counting in odd time. In 3/4 you would count "1 2 3, 1 2 3," usually playing the kick on 1 and the snare on 3, while subdividing the hi-hat groove into the eighth-notes with the lead hand. You normally count the eighth-note subdivision throughout: "1 & 2 & 3 &." This would work well with songs like "In Christ Alone," "Amazing Grace," and "Great Is Thy Faithfulness."

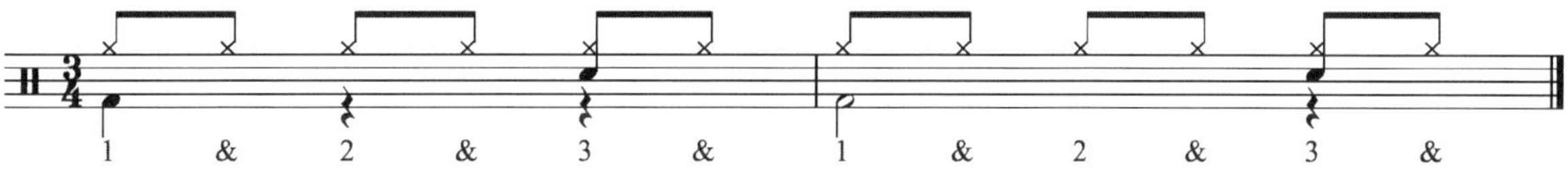

Figure 11.24. A basic 3/4 groove.

As we've done with the other patterns, feel free to add kick notes as you like. Also play filler or ghost notes within the pattern to create a different feel to the groove. For instance, on "In Christ Alone," I normally add the notes in the next figure as a starting point, and even more as the song builds.

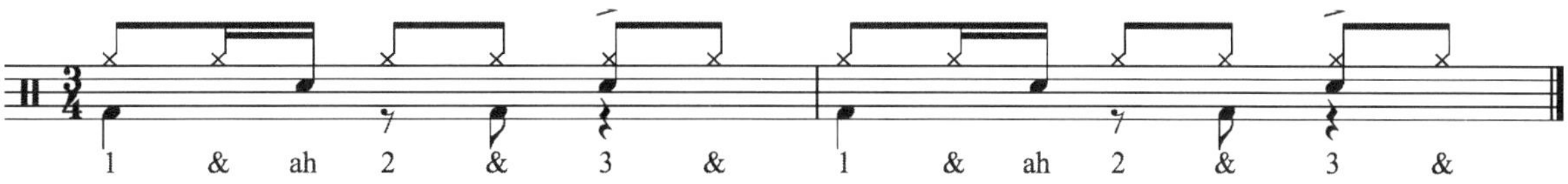

Figure 11.25. Adding notes to the 3/4 groove.

Playing in five is a little harder. I normally break the five counts into phrases according to the feel of the song. In "How Deep the Father's Love," it's felt in a group of three plus two. Count "1_ah 2 & 3&, 1_ah 2 &," or you could say the numbers four and five and count it: "1_ah 2 & 3 &, 4_ah 5 &," and so on. The idea in odd meters is to make it feel as relaxed and natural as you do when playing standard time signatures. Start slow, and count out loud all of the time until you feel comfortable. Eventually you can just count it in your head if you need to. You can also change the ride pattern to a sixteenth-note feel if it helps keep the groove solid.

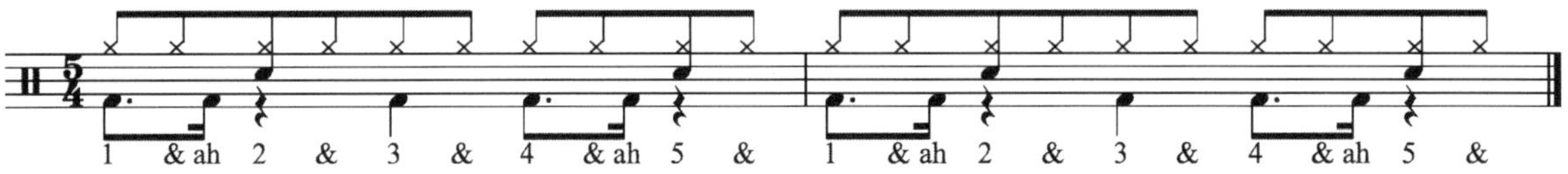

Figure 11.26. A basic 5/4 groove.

There you go! Seven drum groove ideas to launch you into your worship drumming experience with confidence. Remember: these are just the foundational patterns. As you learn more songs, be sure to pay close attention to the details of each one, and copy what you hear the drummer playing on the recordings. I pray this will be a useful primer in your preparation for modern worship drumming.

God bless your grooves!

12

Charts for Drummers

I believe drummers should know how to read music. Even though in modern worship we never use actual drum music, it's important to be able interpret scores, charts, or whatever you are given as the musical map for songs. Today I'm going to look at several types of song charts that you may come across in your musical journeys.

When there is no music available, I'll do a quick sketch chart like the one shown in Figure 12.1 for the song "You Are the One." What you'll see in all the charts is a tempo marking and groove description at the top left. Also look for the time signature so you know how to count. This is what I see first when looking at a chart. These are the most important elements for a drummer to know. It gets the musical feel going in your head right away. I'll always start the metronome and sing the song in my head before I count it off for the band. I also lightly tap the groove on my leg to get the drum feel internalized. As you and your band become more familiar with songs, you can usually just start the click and count off the song and go. The more you play together and perform songs over and over, the more they do become second nature.

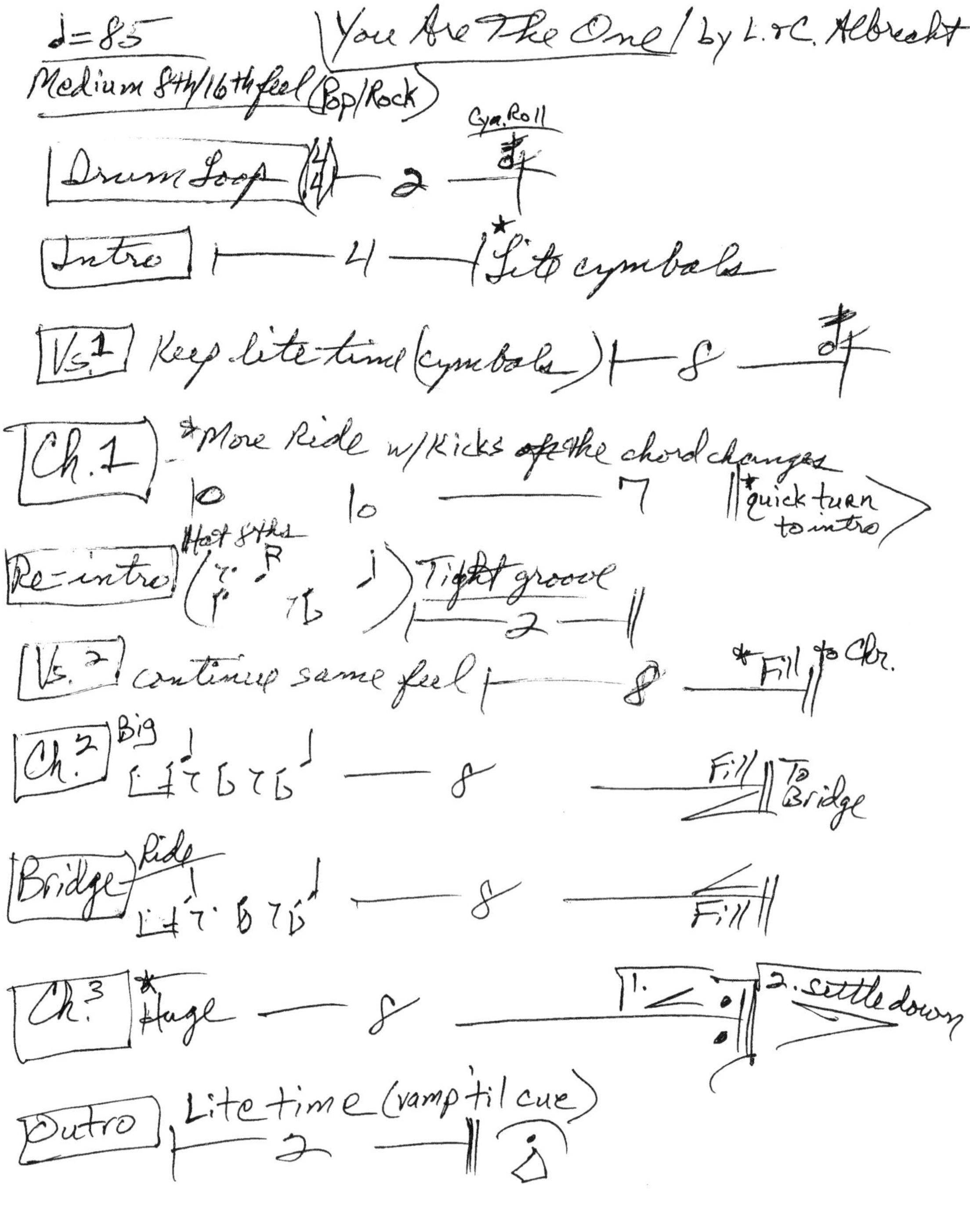

Figure 12.1. Song sketch.

The Sketch

In the sketch version, I just count the number of bars (measures) and try to get the form of the song laid out quickly. The intro is two bars of a drum loop and then a four-bar phrase with a soft cymbal swell at the end of the phrase. Then there's just some light time keeping for the first verse. I often play something very lightly, like soft tapping on the hi-hat or ride cymbal, to help keep the tempo solid. This will definitely happen when I am the only one hearing the click track, but on this song, there is a drum loop playing.

At chorus 1, I should still play softly, but maybe something with a groove going. Then the drums come in stronger at verse 2. I've written one bar of the groove, so I know exactly what to play. I know to use eighth-notes as the main right-hand feel, because it's shown in the groove description at the top of the sketch. The second chorus is a slightly different pattern with a snare backbeat. I will write in as many details and cues as I need, so that I can get the song right every time we play it. The numbers in each line just tell me how many bars are in the section. This works great for learning a song quickly. You can come up with your own version, but this style works well for me.

The Lyric Sheet with Chords

My least favorite song chart is the lyric sheet with chords. This is probably what you see most of the time with your worship teams. It's okay for songs that you know really well and just want to sing along with, but it is very difficult to use to learn new songs and write in specific forms and rhythmic ideas. There's usually not a lot of room to work with, and you just have to make the best of it. See what I did with this one. You can tell I have to squeeze the musical ideas into this type of music.

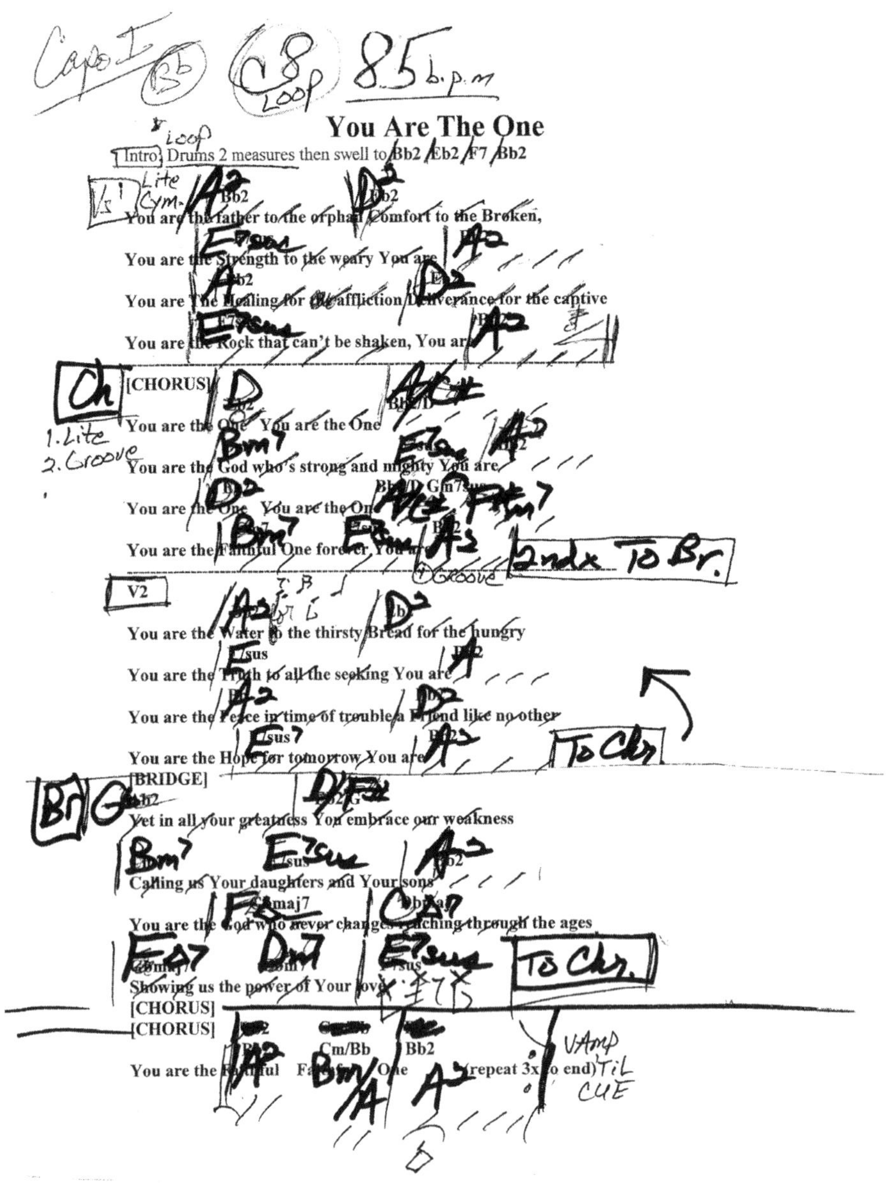

Figure 12.2. Lyric sheet with chords.

When I have to use a lyric sheet, I try to sketch musical concepts around the lyrics. I even show a large slash to indicate the beginning of each measure, and then lighter slashes to show counts. Then I'll write in drum ideas as best as I can. This makes the lyric sheet as much of a musical score as it can be.

At the top are still the same important key elements, but with this tune, we played to loops, so I made a huge note to be sure I would focus on that. I'll remind the band that we're playing to tracks if they don't already know, so that everybody locks into it. It's still tricky to follow a lyric-sheet chart when you're actually playing the tune, but you have to make the best of it. The chord symbols sometime don't land in the right places, and the spacing of things can be very unmusical. You just have to come up with a system that will make it work for you. And this writing in of bar lines and counts has made this workable for me.

A Rhythm Chart

In most worship music, it is very rare to see actual drum scoring. You will see some band charts done with drum ideas sketched in, but nothing that will look like an actual transcription for the drums. For most band situations, it's nice to have a basic rhythm chart. It's similar to a lead sheet, but it doesn't usually have the lyrics like we have here.

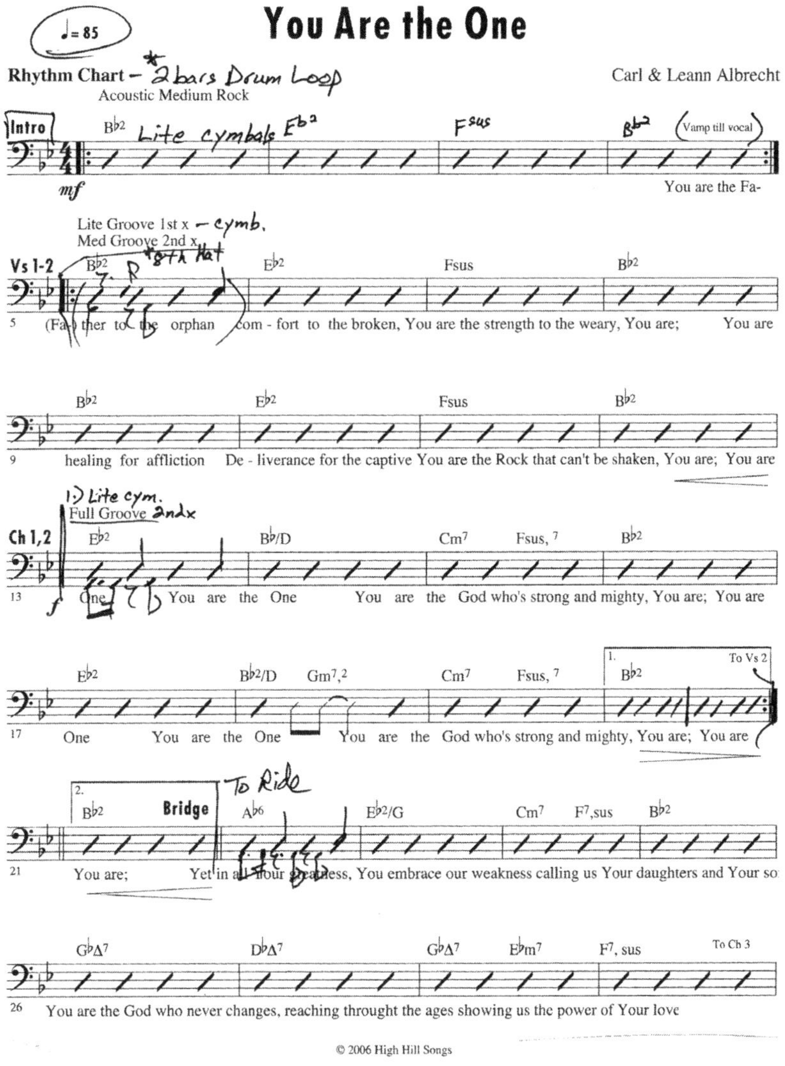

Figure 12.3. Rhythm chart.

The letters written over the bars show the band what chords to play. You can also easily show counts and rhythmic pushes in this kind of chart. Even though there are no drum parts shown, it's easy to write ideas in a score like this. For more intricate tunes, this allows the arranger or you to write in whatever is needed for the correct interpretation of the song. Plus you are able to know exactly where chords land in the bar, and how many measures and phrases are part of the song. As a drummer, I'm able to write in exact drum notation with groove and fill ideas as much as needed. I love this kind of chart.

The Song Lead Sheet

The song lead sheet is also an actual form chart on staff paper with chords, melody, and lyrics added. With this type of chart, you can see the actual melody of the song, as well as some musical notation that other instruments are playing, like the chord pushes you see in bar 5 of the chart. I'll write drum ideas right on top of the other notation. You can see that the intro starts with the drum loop. Then in the next four bars, I add some light cymbal work to the mix. As it enters the first verse, the energy stays down. If I play something different for a repeat section, I'll indicate a number *1* for the first time through, and write above the staff. For the second time through, I'll write a *2* and make my notes below the staff if there is room, even writing over the lyrics when needed.

You Are the One

Words & Music by
CARL and LEANN ALBRECHT

Figure 12.4. Lead sheet.

Using a lead sheet or rhythm chart is really the best way for musicians to learn new songs and build a usable library of material. But keep everything! When possible, I keep every chart from sessions and tours. I highly recommend you do the same. If I have to prepare for a new tour or a leader calls for something we haven't played in a while, I can pull out the charts and relearn things very quickly. Especially with a worship team with many players, it helps the next drummer coming in to know what to do. He or she will at least have a workable chart to use as a reference. Yes, I do have a large filing cabinet, and you should have some way to file your work too. Believe me, it really is a time saver.

If you don't know how to read, I highly recommend getting with a teacher and adding this skill to your talent list. You don't have to be an ace sight-reader to have this musical tool work well for you. Start with whatever musical charts your band uses now, and build from there.

Happy charting!

13

Tricks for Clicks

Question: How do you know when a drummer is knocking at your door?
Answer: The knocking speeds up! Or slows down! Or maybe both!

Sorry gang, I just had to throw that in there. It's one of the many drummer jokes that we get bombarded with. But may it not be true of you! So how do we avoid the problem of shifting tempo? How can you get your time rock steady?

You've guessed it; today's discussion is about the famous click track, a term used to literally describe the track on a tape or computer recording system that is dedicated solely to the metronome. The concept was first developed in film production when they wanted to align musical cues with the action that was happening onscreen. The conductor would listen to a click track printed directly onto the audio portion of a film and conduct the orchestra to match what was happening in the movie. Then it became a staple in studio recording. Now we use it for live playing as much as we do for studio work.

The Click Is Here to Stay

Playing with a click or metronome is one of the biggest challenges for musicians. From my early years of study on drums, percussion, and piano, all of my teachers required that I practice with this tool of the trade. And so it is today. I use it for everything! Practicing, recording, and live events all get the same attention to the mark of the metronome. The bpm (beats per minute) rule the drummer's life. I've played with clicks, clacks, pops, beeps, dings, and many other sounds. So let me show you a few tricks to make this experience more enjoyable. Hopefully this will help you and the whole band feel like the click track is your friend.

What Sound Is Best for the Click

Ultimately you should be able to listen to whatever is sent to you as a click sound. The old electronic pop or high thump is still very popular when playing on a recording session with live orchestras. They like the old popping sound. I think it's reminiscent of the old electronic metronomes with lights on top made by the Franz or Seth Thomas companies. The main thing is to be the team player and don't complain. But if you can be the one who creates the click, then make it something you want to hear all day.

I normally like to have a soft-sounding high cowbell sound on the quarter-notes and then use a small shaker for the subdivisions of the beat. Some want a different sound on the quarter-note or pulse of the song. Other players I've talked to like to hear just a shaker playing eighth-notes, sixteenths, or triplets depending on the feel of the tune. Be careful with the sound of the shaker you use for a click. There are times the sample hits a little strangely and it doesn't sound steady. That's why I normally choose a short-snap shaker sound. Wow! Say *that* fast four times: "Short-snap shaker sound."

Which Metronome

There are so many metronome devices on the market today there's no excuse for all musicians not have one. I just got a music distributor's catalog in the mail today, and the whole back cover is full of metronomes. There was a basic $11 mini–digital metronome, a multifunctional Yamaha ClickStation that listed for $189, and everything else in between. There are even free software metronomes for your Mac or PC. And yes, there's even an app for that:

Mac: http://www.macupdate.com/app/mac/21708/metronome/.
PC: http://www.nch.com.au/metronome/index.html.

If you can spend a little more, I highly recommend getting one of the little drum machines rather than an ordinary metronome. In stores everywhere and online, there are always drum machines for sale. You can easily spend under $200 and get a machine that will work great. An Alesis SR-16 is an excellent inexpensive machine. You can even use a foot switch or a trigger pad to start and stop it. I keep the switch by the heel of my hi-hat pedal. I like to use the percussion sounds that I can program rather than a plain click or beep sound. The main point is to start with something that works for your budget. There's just no reason not to have a metronome.

Learning to Play to the Click

The first time you play to a click can be a very frustrating experience. I recommend starting with the metronome playing double time. In other words, if you want to play something at 80 bpm, set your device to play 160 bpm, and so on. If your machine can play the subdivided notes, then you can easily keep the main pulse at 80, and then let the other sound play double time. For example, you could have a cowbell on quarter-notes and the shaker on eighth-notes. Listen and count for several bars before you start to play. "1 2 3 4; 1 2 3 4"; then begin. We call this internalizing the time. Stay very relaxed and keep your strokes smooth. Don't allow any stiffness in your arms, wrists, or fingers. If you feel your tempo is wandering a little, don't tense up. Just try to feel the pulse and lock into it. If you get totally lost, *stop!* Breathe, start counting again, internalize the time, and start again. You should feel your ears and hands locking into the sound of the click.

I always tell my students not to think of a click as isolated blips, but as long notes that are connected. Picture in your mind the bouncing ball image. "Follow the bouncing ball!" If you think of clicks and all percussion sounds as having length, it should be easier to keep the proper tempo spacing in your playing. I had one teacher tell me to think of the pulse of music as being round, not pointed or square. In musical terms, we would say think legato, not staccato. Whatever picture you can use to get this idea, hang onto it. It really does work!

Keep the Click in Your Headphones

I would also use earbuds or headphones to listen to the click. Most metronomes have a headphone plug. Use it! In most band settings, this is the way you should monitor the sound anyway. Don't send the click sound through the speakers. If you have to, get your own small headphone mixer.

Again, these are easily found in music stores and catalogs. In one channel I have the monitor line sent to me. If possible I like the sound tech to mix in stereo. If that is an option, then they need to send two lines to my mixer. I send my click line into a totally separate channel. And if I'm using drum loops, that is also in a separate channel from the click and mix sends. Having the music mix and the click in separate channels allows you to adjust levels according to the moment. In softer songs, you can turn the click down, but when everything is loud, you might need to turn it up.

I've learned the hard way that not having control of the click level can lead to a musical disaster. When I first started doing this, there were several events where I could not hear the click at a certain moment, and I would lose track of the time. The band would be playing louder and pulling on the tempo, and I would naturally play with them, but it would cause me to not play right with the click. It wasn't long before I learned to get my own mixer to solve that problem.

If I do not have the option to use my own mixer, I will ask the engineer to send me the click at a much higher volume in my headphones, so that I know the music will never cover it. This can be very annoying if you have to listen to a loud click the whole time you are playing. But do what you must to keep your tempos steady.

A Click for Everything

I use a click for everything. Besides always using it on the job, I use a click when practicing rudiments and snare and drum-kit studies, and even when I'm soloing. At least 95 percent of my drum work out is with a metronome or drum machine.

Try different ways of using the click. I'll set up only a quarter-note pulse for some exercises. If I'm mixing the subdivisions of the beat, I don't want the machine playing them for me. It might be interesting to hear triplets against sixteenth-notes, but sometimes I really want to focus on just the main pulse. If the primary feel is heavy with a certain subdivision, then I will allow that to keep playing.

For the opposite approach, try playing with a click only on the offbeats. Rather than hearing the quarter-note pulse, only hear the "and" of the beat when playing eighth-note patterns, or the "and ah" part of the beat if you are playing a sixteenth-note feel. Try other variations of this concept. If you use a drum machine, program a pattern that accents the notes you don't play. When you do this, you really get a feel for how well you are grooving around the time, because you can hear the other notes: the ones that you're not playing. You should think of the machine as another player and begin to relax as you play along with the click. Again, let me emphasize the word *relax*! Stay loose! Tension will make your time feel stiff. You've got to breathe and keep your body movements smooth.

Other Tricks

Other tricks for the click that are fun would consist of leaving beats out. Have the machine click 1, 2, 3, but rest on 4. Try any variation of this you'd like. You could also count the clicks as only sounding on beats 2 and 4, and you have to place the 1 and 3 in the gaps along with all the patterns you are trying to play. I got that idea from my friend Don Harris, an outstanding bass player with impeccable time. By the way, he always practices with a metronome too. Don said that because he felt the bass was normally on the downbeats, hearing the click on the backbeats would make him aware of the feel of his playing against what would sound like the drummer smacking the snare on 2 and 4.

If you play with a basic click on quarter-notes, try keeping the volume of the machine down. When your time is perfect, you won't even hear the click. We call that burying the click. This is also a great way to tell when you're playing *on top*, which means being a little ahead of the click, or *laid back*, which is slightly behind the click. Mentally you almost feel like the machine is rushing or dragging, but believe me, it's you, not the click, that's moving. Don't become tense when you hear this. Concentrate, and become aware of your feel of the time. There are musical settings when you want to change where you feel the tempo. The key is to learn what it feels like and be able to control it at will. A little pushing and pulling can be very musical, but keep it smooth. Never let it feel like you're jerking the time around. Again, I can't emphasize this enough, but it is crucial to relax! If you start using a click every day, you should notice your time improving.

A Click for Everyone

Hopefully all the musicians in your group will start doing this as part of their routine as well. In fact, I think it's good to recommend it. Just be sure to do it in a very positive way. Like you're all agreeing to lift weights or work out together so you can be in tip-top shape. But even if no one else does, do it for yourself and for the sake of the music. Your team will notice the difference. That in itself may be enough to encourage everyone to join you in the discipline of the click.

Maybe you can suggest that everyone use a headphone monitoring system and listen to the click with you. Even if they do that just at rehearsals, it will help. I know several groups that first thought playing with a click would be impossible, but now have gotten so comfortable with it that they use it all the time. It's amazing how the whole band will improve their time as you all play along to your friend the click track.

Okay, say it with me, "The click is my friend!"

14

Drummers! Get a Grip

The discussion on proper drumstick grip just keeps going, and going, and going! In fact not long ago, there was a major write-up about stick-grip techniques in *Modern Drummer* magazine. It was the January 2006 issue, if you'd like to check it out. By the way, you should be subscribing to that publication as well. I feel it is the drummer's most comprehensive resource for drum and percussion information. And no, they did not pay me to say that. I always recommend it to my students and seminar attendees.

So why am I trying to write another commentary on the subject? Well for one thing, repetition is one of the greatest ways to learn. Second, some of you may not read the magazine. And third, I hope to summarize some of the intense and somewhat lengthy debate that was in that issue. Reading that article almost overwhelmed and frustrated me. And I've been doing this a while!

Don't misunderstand me. I'm not saying I have all the answers here, but I have studied a lot. My goal is to summarize all of the ideas into the fundamental concepts that work across the board. Quite often I see drummers struggle with getting a great sound or playing comfortably. Understanding the basics of good stick technique will help with those problems.

Matched or Traditional Grip or…

I use both matched and traditional grip with many variations. This happens according to the music I'm playing and the sound I want to create. For most situations I use matched grip. See Figure 14.1. Yes, those are my hands.

Figure 14.1. Matched grip.

I pinch the stick between the meat of the thumb and the first crook of the first finger. The other three fingers gently wrap around the stick. Keep a firm grip, but not too tight. Just enough pressure to maintain control is all you need. In fact, there are times during practice I try to relax so much that I drop the sticks just to discover my looseness limit.

Normally I keep my hands totally on top of the sticks. This is a German-style approach to stick grip (as it is known in the classical world). This may have come from my university studies with symphonic players, but it also seemed to happen naturally when I played rock and pop music.

I might switch to a thumbs-up technique for a lighter, more finessed approach, which is known as the French grip, or even a little turn of the wrist somewhere between the two techniques. That is probably an influence from my studies with different drum-set teachers. See, I'm already messing with the concepts! See Figure 14.2 for a basic French grip.

Figure 14.2. French grip.

There's not really one right way to hold the sticks. It just seems to be an adjustment you make as you go from thinking technically about music to the actual emotional reactions you have when playing. But it's important to note the effect these different grips have on your sound. That's the most important element to using different approaches to your stick technique. How does it make you sound? What is it doing to the music? Listen carefully, and take note of what each position does to the sound of your drum kit.

I may even switch to traditional grip when the mood strikes. Usually something more delicate and soft needs to be played when I do this. Playing jazz styles often leads me to play this way, but it is not the only time.

Figure 14.3 Traditional grip.

Occasionally I just want to sound a little different. Changing my grip makes me play differently and creates a variety of tones in my sound. But I have to practice with each grip to be sure I can control it. I want to know what the sounds will be when I change the way I hold the sticks, brushes, or anything.

What Is Common to All Grips

Whatever grip I use, I find there are some common denominators in all of them. Even though a drummer needs to be in control of the sticks, one should never use more energy or tightness than necessary. In fact, this is my first comment with students. *Stay relaxed!* Don't grip so tight that your fingers or knuckles turn white. Keep just enough pressure on the sticks to maintain control. That's it! In the *Modern Drummer* article, someone even commented, "Looseness is close to godliness." Of course this only applies to your grip, not your life!

Maintaining finger contact with the sticks at all times is also a factor that applies to every grip. Do not allow them to just flop around in your hands as you play. This is not relaxing. It is just sloppy technique and will not give you a consistent sound on the drums, because the sticks are not striking in the same focused area of the instrument. This is what I call "sloppy looseness." It hinders your ability to play smoothly and in time. So stay in touch with the sticks at all times, but again, only as much pressure as needed.

Use your wrists and fingers as the focus of your stroke. Do not play with a locked or stiff wrist. This will force you to use too much elbow action. You may have seen the wind-up toy monkey that plays the drums. You do not want to look like that when you play. It looks cute on the toy, but it's terrible for a real drummer.

If I need more volume, I'll use a whipping motion of the arm to get more power. But at the end of the stroke, it's always a snap of the wrist and a slight pulling of the fingers that makes the sound. Try it right now. Pretend you're a circus lion tamer cracking a whip. That's the motion you go for when needing more power in your playing.

Finally, be sure to keep all of your strokes smooth. Some teachers describe this as a fluid motion. This again is a reference to being relaxed when you play. A drummer's physical movements should almost resemble the floating quality of a ballroom dancer. In fact there have been several great drummers who studied dancing to help their playing. You don't have to do that, but you must develop this concept in your playing style.

When I do my practice routine, I always make time to study my grip. I'll remember these common rules even as I switch my grip from one type to another. I switch grips as I'm playing rudiments or grooves just to see what effect it has on my sound and the steadiness of my time. Yes, the metronome will be playing all the while to be sure my timing is steady. I know you've heard me say this before. You should know it by now. "The metronome is our friend!" I also change up the dynamics of my exercises when using all of the grips. You have to be able to control the sticks whether the volume is soft, medium, or loud.

Use the Mirror

Another great tool is a mirror. No, I don't like to look at myself. I use it to watch my technique when I'm playing. I set up wall mirrors in front of the kit and to the sides so I can watch my hands, wrists, arms, and feet. I basically try to observe my whole body posture and movement as I play. I even know players who would put mirrors on the floor so they could see their hands from underneath. This is an awesome tool. You get an immediate picture of what you are really doing. There are times I can see in the mirror something I need to adjust in my technique to fix a problem.

For instance, one time I noticed my hand was reaching too far to strike a certain crash cymbal. By changing the angle and height of the cymbal, I noticed my arm did not strain as much. What a great teacher a mirror can be. But I am also a strong believer in studying with a qualified teacher to enhance your drum studies. No matter what level of player you are, you should keep looking for ways to grow and for those that can help you accomplish that.

Tony Williams, a great drum icon, once made this statement concerning drum technique: "It's a lifelong endeavor." I agree totally! It's good to learn all that you can so you can become the best musician God made you to be. Just remember that these are the tools of your trade. Learn how to use all of the tools, but don't get so caught up in the technique that you forget to let the music pour out of your spirit. I believe people hear your soul, not your hands. In the end, that's what makes all the difference.

15

Drumming for the Song

Ah yes, another seminar and concert event has finished. Great teaching sessions and nights of worship have been followed with many discussions about technical and spiritual matters. Questions about how to tune the drums or what equipment I prefer are fairly common. Also comments about how certain songs touched people or the positive team spirit of the band are heard. But the most popular topic here, by far, is the busy drummer syndrome. This doesn't mean keeping the calendar full of appointments either. No, sadly, I frequently talk with worship leaders, music directors, and other musicians about their drummers overplaying.

Play the Song

Drummers, here's the deal! Most people don't want to hear a fill every two bars. They don't care how hard you've practiced to play those 32nd-note patterns or to nail the solo from your favorite drum recording. They just want you to *play the song!* Keep the tempo steady, and play the tune the way you hear it on the recording, *and that's it!* The italics mean that I'm shouting! Oh, I'm sorry. I mean, speaking with a strong emphasis. Actually, I'd pull my hair out except that I shave my head now and have nothing left to grab. Why is it that so many drummers don't get this? It is a mystery.

You may have heard me say this before, but it's worth repeating. I always tell my students and clinic attendees to "Play music, not just drums!" Serving the song and your team is your primary objective. If you think the songs are supposed to serve you and give you a way to show off your sweet drumming skills, you've got it all wrong!

Now I know I'm making a big deal out of this, but it is a big deal. Making the song sound great is every musician's job. If that is your heart about being a drummer, people will love your playing. If the music calls for a lot of activity, then go for it. But if it's just playing grooves for tunes, then master that skill as well.

What Great Drummers Do

Every great drum icon I've seen and heard made the whole band sound fantastic. Especially when working with singer/artist types of performers, they always play for the song. And it is always a magical experience. Take some time to watch video clips of Steve Gadd playing for James Taylor or Eric Clapton, Vinnie Colaiuta playing for Sting or Faith Hill, or any other drumming virtuoso just laying down a fat groove for an artist. It's totally inspiring!

Drummers often think that their drum heroes must be very restrained in their ability to just play songs. I've heard them say, "They must be bored out of their mind! I wish they could really cut loose!" But you know, the regular people listening never think of it like that. The nonmusician folks are just enjoying and experiencing the music. They just love to hear their favorite songs.

Keep It Simple

So how do you keep from becoming infected with the busy drummer syndrome? The first thing I do is just copy what has already been done. Listen to the original recordings, and just do what they do. It's that simple. And yes, *simple* is usually the operative word. Most songs are arranged very carefully. Check out any of your favorite artists or worship recordings, and you'll hear what I mean. The intro, verses, choruses, and bridge of the song all seem to have specific musical ideas happening. Play it just like that.

Yeah, I know what you're thinking, "But Carl, that's sooooooo boring! I want to add some flash to it, put some of my own personality into it! Man, I've got to express myself!" Arghhhhhhhhh! Get over this attitude as soon as possible. Express your personal stuff at home! Blow off that creative drive during your practice time. Otherwise, just play the songs. Doing a great job, by the way, is the proper way to express yourself. It is the most mature thing you can do as a musician. Making great music and bringing the songs to life is what it's all about. There is not one artist that I've worked with that doesn't feel the same way about this subject.

Ask About Your Playing

Another way to battle this illness is to talk to your worship leader or music director and ask if what you're playing is working for them. If you've started with the recording as your reference, they'll usually like what you are doing. But there are times they do want a little more activity just to add energy to certain songs. Don't get carried away though. This is not permission for you to become a drum monster. You know, you've seen them in movies, the big creatures stepping on everything that gets in their way. Yes, you must ask the people you work with about how it feels to them. Sometimes people are afraid to talk to you about your playing because everyone knows how sensitive musicians can be. And drummers are usually very mysterious creatures to the other players and singers in a group.

Record Your Work

Recording your rehearsals and performances is also a great tool in learning more about your playing. Video record it if you can, but do something to archive your performance so you can go back and check out how it went. Be honest with yourself, and make note of both your great and bad moments. Let others review your recording as well. Then change anything you need to in order to make your performance even better.

Finally, practice groove ideas with a click track for eight bars without any changes. I call this "playing eights." I heard about this, years ago, from an interview someone did with the drum icon Steve Gadd. I figure if it helped Steve, it can help all of us. Only do fills at the end of the eight-bar phrase, and then go to a variation of the groove for the next section. Do not even do fills in the fourth measure. Play for at least four to five minutes at one tempo, and build on one particular groove concept. This is an exercise in restraint. It will really help your groove become solid, because you're just focusing on time and feel. It's not physically difficult, but it can be a real mental challenge. Do it!

Listen closely to how consistent you are with every element of your playing. Do the snare hits sound exactly alike? Is your hi-hat pattern maintaining a steady pace? Does the bass drum perfectly line up with your hands and sound solid? Put your playing under the microscope, and perfect every element to the best of your ability.

Okay, so you say you've heard it all before. Great! But are you doing it? Are you really honing in on your musical artistry? Do not become complacent or rest on yesterday's accomplishments. Keep moving ahead. Improve what talent you already have. So here's your groove checklist.

1. Copy the drummers on great recordings.
2. Ask for honest feedback from those you work with.
3. Record yourself all of the time and review it.
4. Practice the eight-bar phrase concept with a click.

Playing simple, great grooves is not as simple you may think. It takes a strong, mature player to do this. But the payoff is amazing. The whole band is going to sound better. Your singers are going to love how open and spacious the tunes feel. And you should feel more confident and solid in your performance. Again, remember it's all about the music. Play what's right for the style of songs you're doing, and you'll be honored among your peers. Play music—not just drums!

16

Worship Drumming Trends

There are no new things on the horizon for worship drummers. And there's nothing you can do about it. Okay, I'm kidding. I just wanted to make sure you were paying attention.

Music and worship are ever changing! Probably because God is covering the Earth with His glory like He said He would do in the scriptures, and worship is part of the plan. He is a very creative God. We just have to stay open to what the Lord is revealing about music, arts, and the worship movement that is unfolding in these times.

For drummers and other musicians, the key is not to allow complacency to infect your creative life. That has happened to me before, and I do everything I can to push back against that enemy. I do all I can to stay fresh and hungry for the Lord and what He has called me to. This applies also to my musical and artistic journey.

Keep Studying, Keep Learning

Sometimes it's a matter of studying new worship songs or styles. Yes, I did say studying! It's foundational to experience the music for the sake of worshipping, but it is also vital and proper to analyze the technical side of songs. Listen to music, and take notes about the mechanics of what's going on. How do the drums sound and feel? How do they fit into the mix with everything else on the recording? Is there a lot of percussion in the track? Are there drum loops and special technical tricks going on as well? Listen intensely to the music as if you could hear in 3-D. Become aware of every dimension of a song.

Modern worship encompasses so many musical forms that you can virtually find God in any kind of music you like. From rock to jazz, from country to classical—it's all there. And that is amazing! Now for sure, the marketing of worship has only focused heavily on the pop-rock styles we are all familiar with. But just so you don't misunderstand what I'm getting at, I happen to like it all! I'm not being critical. This is not about slamming the industry that has promoted contemporary Christian music and gotten on the worship bandwagon. I know the industry gets wrapped up in working popular formulas, but the art still keeps evolving, even if it does feel slow to some people.

Keep Your Ears Open

For the sake of the art of drumming and all other musical expressions, keep your ears and your mind open. If you feel stale and uninspired, listen to some country gospel. Yep, that too! Then listen to some big band worship and play along. How often do you get to work on your swing feel? Maybe also try some Latin or salsa worship. Definitely work on the modern worship stuff that is popular right now. But work on that slammin' urban gospel vibe too. And so it goes, on and on. The learning and growing should be a lifelong journey.

In the past couple of months, I have recorded drum and percussion tracks for a huge variety of worship styles. Classical, classic rock, jazz, and country, just to list a few. If I wasn't listening and working on these musical flavors, I could not do the work. So drummers, get back in the woodshed and sweat your way through some fresh music. Not just new songs in general, but playing styles that you are not used to playing.

Many Trends

So what are the trends? There is not only one. Many musical expressions are exploding around the world. Sometimes it's easy to get trapped in a musical whirlpool where you can't see what else is happening. Thanks to digital musical servers, it's easier to find the obscure artistic expressions. So dive in and see what your God is doing on the Earth. Note: At random, I just jumped over to my iTunes store and sampled Randy Travis singing a country version of "Open the Eyes of My Heart." Very cool!

When studying the trends of modern worship, be aware of the flavor of the drum sounds you are hearing. Are they big, fat, rockin' drums, or do they sound tighter, higher pitched, and snappy? The trend or challenge for us as drummers is to be more like musical parrots. Drummer wanna' cracker? Awwk! Yeah, eat it all up. Absolutely listen to the latest from all the modern worship icons. Just don't get stuck there. It's okay to have your favorites, but be sure to work your other musical muscles. Expand your musical territory.

Create Challenges

A good way to challenge yourself is to change your drum setup each week. Play a stripped-down kit for a week—a kick, snare, hi-hat, one tom, a ride cymbal, and a crash cymbal. Next week, add one tom. The next week move your cymbals around. Later, you might even try setting up a huge drum set. Yes, I really do this. On this current tour, I'm playing a basic five-piece kit with the addition of a brass piccolo snare to the left of the hi-hat because the music calls for it. A ride, hi-hats, and two crashes are all the cymbals I'm using. The sizes of the drums are a 22-inch kick; 10-, 12-, and 16-inch toms; a 14-inch by 5-inch maple snare, and a 13-inch by 3-inch brass piccolo snare. My studio kit uses four toms and tons more cymbals, but they're set up in an unusual configuration. I keep mixing things up just so I have to think about what I'm doing. Yes, I am careful to keep everything placed comfortably so I can play smoothly, but there are so many possibilities.

Be creative and try new types of drumheads, new sticks, new muffling techniques, and so on. Okay, you've got the idea. Now run with it! Send me an e-mail and let me know what happens to your playing as you stretch your creative muscle. Keep those cards and letters comin'! Frequently, I write articles or respond to something someone has asked me about on my website.

17

Everyone Depends on the Drummer

So it didn't feel so good tonight. The grooves didn't lock in; the arrangements were off; even the singers didn't blend as well. Oh yeah, and the mix felt weird. It must be the drummer's fault! I know this is an old band joke, but sometimes it feels that way. We drummers often feel like we're being blamed for a lot of things that are out of our control.

The truth is, the drummer does carry a lot of responsibility to lead the band. How confidently we play and how well we lead a band through the flow of a song is a huge part of playing great music. We must, at all times, play with confidence and power. This, by the way, does not mean playing louder than everyone else. And it also does not mean acting like an arrogant fool.

Confidence Under Pressure

What brought me to this discussion is something I experienced recently at a festival in Lagos, Nigeria. I was playing for Don Moen, Ron Kenoly, and Phil Driscoll at an all-night worship event with many artists, musicians, speakers, and preachers. In fact it was called "The Experience," and it certainly was! It was estimated that we were worshipping with over 500,000 people. I think it's the largest gathering I've ever played for. The event started at seven p.m. and was scheduled to go until seven a.m. the next morning. It was a very emotional and powerful gathering of God's people.

Because Phil had not brought a band, he asked some of the other players to sit in with him. He would mostly use tracks, but he wanted us to play along with them to add power to the tunes. He also wanted to be able to flow into other worship songs and minister as the band played. No rehearsal! No hearing the tunes ahead of time! I was okay with that, because I know he just wanted a flow of music and musicians that would worship with him. It was a very powerful moment.

Technically speaking, I was listening intensely to the tracks as we played along—as if I were anticipating where the music would go and how it would build. Thank God the songs seem to have a natural or common structure that seemed to make the task a little easier. No train wrecks occurred—the worship flowed. As Phil moved into spontaneous songs of worship, he led the team well through the journey. His cues were excellent, and everyone was very attentive. I recall thinking that years of training and playing thousands of songs were paying off with good results. Drummers take special note here. I said *years of training* and *playing thousands of songs*. That's very important!

Knowing You're Called

The other thing that struck me was that I wasn't afraid, but comfortable with taking on such a strange task. Playing without any preparation. Crazy! But knowing what the Lord has given me to do on the Earth and being aware of my schooling and experience gave me confidence to say yes. By the way, this is not to say that I felt proud. I just knew the Lord would be with us. And yes, I believe His Spirit was upon us for the thing He called us to. At the end of his set, Phil was very pleased, and grateful for our attentiveness, boldness, and sensitivity to the flow of worship.

Next was my role as drummer for Ron Kenoly. Even though I've worked with him before, it had been a long, long time. I had a chance to look through his music at the hotel before the event, but that was all. Some of the arrangements were pretty complex, and I made my markings on the charts as quickly as I could. Again, no rehearsal! Fortunately, having played on many of Ron's recordings, I did find the music familiar. As I watched the charts and listened to the songs, I played air drums to get a feel for the music. There was no time to get into a practice room somewhere or rehearse on the stage before the sound check.

At the concert that night, I got through the first tune without a hitch. But during the second song, a medley of "Jubilee" and "Mourning into Dancing," I was so excited hearing the band and watching Ron lead us through a great time of worship that I lost my place in the chart. I missed a few cues and hits with the horns. Bummer! But I never stopped the flow of the groove, and we just kept cruising along. No train wrecks! Just not as smooth as I would have liked it.

Don't Get Distracted

I thought to myself, "You can never let yourself get distracted from the task at hand. Stay focused, even in the midst of extreme emotion." Drummers take note again: We are always serving the team. Don't get caught up in your own experience.

I realize playing in front of 500,000 people can affect anyone. And having a great time of worship with your friends can get your guard down. But it's always important to remember you are there to serve and to do the job a drummer should do. You are driving the bus—musically speaking, of course. Which just means you must keep good time and hold the band together. Lead them through the sections of the songs clearly, and play with confidence.

Next I played for Don Moen. I have worked with Don for years and played on many of his recordings. So I'm pretty comfortable with the job. But on this tour, half of the band was relatively new to the gig, and our sound check had been pretty minimal. I made sure this time that my click track was clear in my headphones and my mix was working well. And even though I've worked with Don a lot, I made sure I was aware of the song list and the flow of the charts.

This was a good move, because as we started the first tune, the band began to look around the stage, realizing the monitor mixes were not as they had been at sound check. Imagine that! Realizing that no one could hear very well, I actually started playing a little more strongly so everyone could feel the time better, and so we plowed through the first song, and then the second song, and so on. As we worshipped, we kept trying to tweak the mix, but it did not seem to help much. We found out later that some of the input lines from the instruments had been switched, as well as some of the mix sends back to the monitors. So the more we tried to fix it, the more we were actually making things worse, and adjusting the wrong mixes as we asked for changes.

Anyway, we just kept playing, smiling, and just getting through the list. Everyone did a great job, and we basically played by faith, because we really could not hear what we were doing. Because I dug in a little more, it helped keep the band together. The house engineer even mentioned that it sounded great out front. Now imagine if we all had lost our confidence and not played to the best of our ability. I'm sure that the congregation would have felt a less passionate musical experience.

This aspect of drumming and general professional musicianship isn't something that can be practiced as much as you learn it over time. But I wanted you to have a picture in your mind, so that as you learn these lessons, it will go deep into your musical character. Also, as a worship drummer, your role carries a priestly aspect of being a minister of music. You are not just keeping time. Lead the way into the presence of the Lord alongside your worship leaders. Don't lose your focus!

18

One Drum Kit, Many Drummers, or "Can We All Just Get Along?!"

I love to play my personal drum kit. It feels right! Everything seems to be perfectly suited to my size and shape. Please, no comments about my size or shape. You know what I mean. You spend hours practicing and playing on the same instrument, and it just seems to become part of you. The drum throne feels like home base. All of the drums and cymbals are in the exact spot that you have meticulously placed them. Everything is adjusted to the microscopic degree of height, angle, and tension. All of the sounds of your kit are an inspiration to the way you play. The music flows naturally. Ahhhhhhh! Beautiful!

The House Kit

Now we go to the church, or a music festival or some other multiple-band event, and there sits the drum kit that all drummers dread: the house kit. These are the drums that are used for every show or that remain in the church all week, and besides the real players, everyone who has an itch to play drums has sat down and made themselves at home with this kit. They pretend to be drummers while beating the poor things to death. If you tour doing fly dates—traveling by airline or playing festivals—it's the rental kit, or what is called the "backline" drums. And believe me, rental drums are "like a box of chocolates; you never know what you're gonna get!"

The most important thing in any situation like this is to keep a good attitude and not become a drum diva. You know, the player that says, "Well, I just can't play on this kit; they are not the hip, cool drums that I use, and they're just not configured the way that I must have them!" Oh, please, please don't ever do that! Just step back and evaluate how to work with what you are given. Stay humble and gracious in every situation, and the people will remember you for that long after the memory of your musical genius has faded.

I realize that it is not as inspiring to play an instrument that may not be up to par with yours. But I believe that inspiration and great music come from your soul, not from your instrument. Here again, I'll admit this can be very challenging. Face this test of your character, and conquer it!

The Church Kit

In the church setting, I get together with all of the other drummers and we have a little chat. Can we talk? Especially in church ministry, we should truly be a band of brothers. Oh, and sisters too, of course, if that applies. We will eventually agree on a setup that we can all play with very little adjusting from one player to the next. I usually recommend that you build from the basic five-piece kit and then go from there. You know: kick drum, snare, two rack toms, a floor tom; then hi-hats, ride cymbal, and two crashes. You might add a second snare to the left of the hi-hat. Maybe another floor tom next to the other one works for everyone. More cymbals can work too, if you can all agree on a common position for them.

In some situations, maybe everyone will prefer a four-piece kit. This old-school setup uses one rack tom, and then the ride cymbal is positioned lower to the kit where the second tom normally sits. This seems to be a common approach for more straight-ahead rock music too. But again, the idea is to come up with a basic setup that all the players can be happy with. Don't be so particular that you can't adjust to a common drum setup.

Go for Little Adjustments

Slight adjustments in drum-throne height or angles of cymbals or drums are understandable, but more radical changes can be a real hassle. For example, changing from a five-piece to a four-piece configuration every time is a big deal. Or moving all of the cymbals around to some personal pattern takes up a lot of time. I understand this could be necessary if there are right-handed and left-handed players. But in most situations, I think we can all come up with a common setup.

In the church music world, you may feel that from service to service there is plenty of time to change a drum set to each player's personal design. That is probably true, but is that really the most efficient way to work? Every player would have to spend more time getting ready at each event he or she played. The engineer would have to reset microphones. And the drum set itself would start to wear out faster because of the constant tweaking it would have to endure.

The Challenge of Music Festivals

At festival concerts, I usually just walk on to the stage with my stick bag and try to sit down and play the drums just as they are set. Maybe a slight throne adjustment, a little drum and cymbal angle change, and away we go.

I won't even change cymbals or the kick pedal unless it just isn't working for me. I do carry mine with me, but I don't always use them. I can just hear someone saying, "Ah, Carl, are you crazy?" Nope! I'm just tryin' to keep my drum life simple.

At these festivals or other multiple-drummer settings, I'm trying to help not only the other players but the technical crew as well. Those gigs are tough. And everyone's working hard. Transitions from one band to the next usually happen very quickly. Many times I've had crew guys thank me for making their lives easier. I just look at it like a learning experience each time. Sometimes it's a great experiment. At other times I have suffered through some bad drum or cymbal sounds. I'll take note of what I was playing that I liked or didn't like. What adjustment was really necessary that I overlooked?

I always attempt to stay positive no matter what happens. Being a "can do" kind of player just makes life more pleasant for everyone. I might even have time to fix broken drums or help change heads if needed. Yes, I've really done that. When transitions are happening fast, I'll usually help the next drummer get set up. Hopefully that drummer will try to play the kit as it has been set up also. This doesn't always happen, but when it does, things just flow better.

When a drummer demands a lot of changes, everyone seems to be a little more stressed out. That's not a good environment to be in at a music festival, and even less so at a Christian music event. It is ultimately a spiritual downer when you're playing for a praise and worship gathering and the players can't cooperate and work together for the common good. To quote our Star Trek hero, Spock: "The needs of the many outweigh the needs of the one." But how about a Scripture?

> *Do nothing out of selfish ambition or vain conceit, but in humility consider others better than yourselves. Each of you should look not only to your own interests, but also to the interests of others.*
>
> —Philippians 2:3–4

The Church World

Most of you doing church ministry don't have to deal with touring or multiple-band events. It's still a challenge to make all the drummers happy with the one drum kit everyone will use week in and week out. I've even heard stories about just two drummers being at odds with each other over this issue. Think of a church where you might have the challenge of three or four or even more players. The bottom line is to find common ground on which everyone can do his or her best. Making the drums functional for everyone with the least amount of changing should be the goal of your drum team. I mean, really, "Can we all just get along?" Get together with all the drummers in your ministry and remember that old ball-team shout: "Teamwork, teamwork, let's go!"

19

Expecting the Unexpected, or "That Would Never Happen to Me!"

For the first time in 25 years of being a professional drummer, I broke a kick drum head all the way through the other night. But *nooooo*, not at sound check or a session where we would just take a break and fix it. It was the first song of the evening in a concert with Paul Baloche! Why can't that sort of thing happen at a convenient time? Inconceivable! And no, I don't believe in Murphy's Law, which says, "If something can go wrong, it will."

Well, I just kept on playing with the kick mallet flopping through the perfectly sliced drumhead. The rest of the band looked at me with that "What are you doing?" sort of look. There had been a definite change in the sound and feel of the music. The next song was supposed to start immediately after the first. So I counted it off and proceeded to play the floor tom with my right hand for the kick pattern and the snare with my left for the backbeats. At the same time, I played eighth-notes on my hi-hat with my left foot. Because the song was in a driving rock style, it actually worked pretty well. Paul turned around and gave me a funny look, and later commented that he thought I was trying to be creative.

While I kept a smile on my face and just poured my heart out in worship, we got through those first couple of songs without falling apart. At the end of the second song, I told Paul what had happened. I ran off the platform and made a beeline for the church choir room.

Know the Venue

Earlier in the day, I had roamed around the building exploring the church, as I often do when we travel. There was an old drum set in the choir room that became my lifesaver for the evening. While Paul shared with the congregation and played a more unplugged tune, I borrowed the bass drum from that old beat-up kit and took it to the stage. In a few seconds, with the help of the sound crew, the drums on the platform were ready to go again. Luckily, in this situation, I did not mount anything on my bass drum, so we were able to quickly slide the damaged one out. I put the old kick drum in place, tuned it, clamped on my pedal; the guys positioned the microphone; and "bam," we were back in business. The rest of the evening was a great time of enjoying the presence of God without technical interruptions.

I have been accused of being too cautious at times. Jokes about all the extra stuff I carry with me are often heard at sessions or on tour.

"Ask Carl, I'm sure he's got it in his bag."

"Anyone got fingernail clippers, a 9-volt battery, a guitar cable, duct tape?"

"Oh, check with Carl."

That night I was so happy to have been thinking of the worst-case scenario. It's not that I'm paranoid, I've just learned to expect the unexpected. Please don't think of this as bragging either. I'm just grateful to those who have taught and taunted me about being ready for anything.

Be Prepared

Go to the job as if no one will have anything you need. That should mean having these things in your stick bag and road cases. I also have spare parts like this at our church.

1. A large supply of sticks, brushes, mallets, and other "weapons" in your bag of varied weights and models for whatever styles you have to play. You might also keep a few pairs of sticks in odd places rather than your stick bag. A good idea would be to keep a pair of sticks in your luggage, another drum case, even your cymbal case. You'll be glad you did if your stick bag is ever lost or delayed in flight.
2. Spare parts for every moving part on your drums: kick pedal springs, straps, nuts and bolts, pins for footboards, and so forth.
3. An extra hi-hat clutch. That's the device that holds the top cymbal of your hi-hat set on the rod of the hi-hat stand. Yes, I have had that piece mysteriously disappear. This can happen at any time, but especially when renting drums on the road.
4. Wing nuts, felt washers, and nylon sleeves for cymbal stands. You can buy a pack of these items at most music stores. Here's a special tip: you can even go to a hardware or auto-parts store and get felt, nylon tubing, and other spare items for much less money.
5. A kick drum head patch pad. On most kick drum heads, especially double-ply heads, you can see a small split begin to happen. Before it becomes the nightmare I described earlier, use a patch at the point of attack. I know the sound is a little different, but in live settings, it will spare you the fun I had the other night. Note: I was using a backline (rented) tour kit without a double-ply head that night.
6. Extra drumheads for each drum.
7. String or straps for your snare drum wires.
8. A few spare drum lugs in case the drum gremlin steals some of yours. They get loose and come out from all the vibrations. They also fall out of the road case never to be found. Go figure!
9. An extra kick drum pedal. It should be one that you can fold down to fit into a tour case or piece of luggage. Even if you have parts, you don't want to take time during a concert to rebuild a pedal. It doesn't have to be expensive. Just get one.
10. And of course—*Dut* da da *da*—a small roll of duct tape! The "quicker fixer upper" for all musicians.

Carry Doubles If You Can

In situations where it's possible, you could carry doubles of everything. The whole drum set is usually duplicated on big tours. This is not the norm for most of the smaller tours or fly dates. Normally I only take three pieces of luggage when flying. My luggage for clothes also contains my stick case. The road case with my cymbals also has a spare kick pedal, small percussion items, heads, and music. These two cases are checked. My third piece is my carry-on with toiletries, my laptop, my mini sampler, a drum machine, some books, and other personal things.

The concert organizer usually supplies the drums and other equipment. If the budget will allow it, I'll bring a case with two snare drums. The airlines are charging a lot more for the extra bags now, so I've been making that a rare option. I only do this when I'm working on a recording or the artist requests it. Again, if it's a bigger tour and there is an equipment truck in the convoy, we'll take doubles of everything.

I always send a very detailed list of things I need for an event or concert. Allowing for supply problems, I give plenty of options if they cannot locate the specific equipment requested. For example, I'll give a list of several snare drum options or even different drum manufacturers so that my drum rider, the contract equipment list, doesn't look like the search for the Holy Grail. I still contact event coordinators to verify that everything is coming together okay on their end. Believe it or not, sometimes they don't even read the contract or equipment riders that artists send.

So the other rule for good preparation is:

Communicate, Communicate, Communicate!

This doesn't require a long list. It's just a principal that I apply to almost everything I do. Communicating well with the team and crew is one of the best things I've learned through the years of touring, session work, and ministry events that has spared me a lot of frustration.

After all of the preparation, I still do the walk-through I mentioned earlier. Just to get an idea of what is available for an emergency. If I'm traveling with all of my own gear, that's not usually a concern. I may still do it just for the fun of exploring. Who knows; the equipment truck might break down or get hijacked by terrorists looking for my drums! Nah, "That would never happen to me!"

20

Still Serving After All These Years

Scriptures (NIV)

> *Whoever wants to become great among you must be your servant . . . just as the Son of Man did not come to be served but to serve.*
>
> —Matthew 20:26–28
>
> *[Jesus] made himself nothing, taking the very nature of a servant*
>
> —Philippians 2:7
>
> *Submit to one another out of reverence for Christ.*
>
> —Ephesians 5:21

Wait, please go back and read these Scriptures again, and meditate upon them in relationship to your calling as a drummer/musician.

I find it very difficult to continue writing anything after reading these Scriptures. Just meditating on them has made me pause and consider the weight of what they say. The Word of God is so powerful and true I really cannot add anything to it. But I will humbly proceed to share my heart on this subject as a musician who has served for years. Read slowly, and chew on these thoughts.

It's amazing how often I hear from worship leaders, pastors, and artists that they are having trouble with a musician's attitude. These frustrated leaders will say, "They can play great, but they are just so hard to deal with!" Always complaining or arguing, and always put out by any request that might be made of him or her, a player like this is a thorn in the side of any music leader. This does not create a great working environment. And it probably works against any sense of unity and teamwork you are trying to build.

In the secular world, a player like this normally gets fired. "Yo! You! You're outta here!" Problem solved. But leaders usually don't do this in ministry situations, because it's more of a family or community environment. I firmly believe that, in the church, we should be willing to ask someone to sit out for a while so he or she can work on some personal issues. That sounds so nice, doesn't it? It could take weeks, maybe months. No matter how difficult this may be, you must deal with it before it becomes a spiritual cancer in your team. Trust me, bad attitudes will either infect or affect everyone. I've seen it happen time and time again.

Is This You?

How do you deal with this if you are the one I'm talking about? What if you've become difficult to work with? Maybe you've lately found it difficult to serve others with your talents. You didn't mean for this to happen. You didn't start out like this—being self-centered and obnoxious. It just seemed to sneak up on you and become part of your persona. Maybe it's from burnout, or a defense mechanism to not get your feelings hurt, or it could be you just have not had good mentoring in relational skills. No one has shown you how to serve. As a drummer/musician who has been asked to serve in many situations and do many different and personally challenging things, let me share some practical ideas. Being challenged on the job is just part of life, and we have to learn how to deal with it.

My best advice is to die to yourself. Anything in your attitude that wants to be self-serving or concerned about your own image has to be put aside. Whatever ministry or job setting I'm in, I always remind myself of why I am there. God has given me gifts and talents to serve those that He connects me to. Unless I am creating my own music or working for myself, my calling and job is to help others find the magic in their music or get a job done. I'm called to help worship leaders and artists find that place where they feel they are able to express their hearts to the Lord and communicate a message to a congregation or audience. I have a mental picture that I am a gatekeeper to the presence of God. Meditate on that image for a while. Take it to heart!

A "Can Do" Person

I know it sounds great in print to be a "can do" person. But how do we really live it? How can we make that happen? Well, to the best of your ability, do what's asked of you at all times. When asked to play softer, play softer. When asked to play less, play less. When asked to show up earlier, be there earlier. When asked to do just about anything, do whatever you can to make it happen. I think you get the picture. I've even had artists ask for different drums or percussion sounds. So I've gone out and bought new equipment to be able to serve them. Sometimes there's a request for a certain kind of look or clothing style. I go out shopping and buy new outfits if needed.

Basically, *I keep trying till I see them smiling.* I haven't always hit the mark when it comes to these things. There are times when you can't seem to please people, but I keep trying. If someone is unhappy with what I'm doing, at least they know I'm giving them my best effort. There are just times when circumstances are out of your control. This is a truth we don't always like to admit.

Ask the Boss How You're Doing

Another thing I do is keep asking questions to be sure leaders or singers are truly getting what they want from me. That will usually diffuse the sense of frustration they may be feeling as they are trying to discover what really works for them. The creative process is often like digging for buried treasure; you might have to sweat a little to get to the gold. That's okay, just keep digging!

A few years ago, we recorded Paul Baloche's CD/DVD called *Offering.* Paul took the time to fly to Nashville for a couple of days with the band just to work out arrangements before the recording dates. In the process of creating, Paul asked me not to use splash cymbals. So I removed them from my kit. Then he asked if I would try not using so many drums. Normally I have four toms in my setup. By the time we were finished, I was down to a four-piece kit: a kick drum, a snare, a 12-inch tom on top of the kick, and a 16-inch floor tom. I did use a second snare (a piccolo snare) to the left of my hi-hat for an alternate backbeat sound as requested. My normal cymbal setup of eight or more was scaled down to a 22-inch ride cymbal, 14-inch hi-hats, an 18-inch crash, a 19-inch rock crash, and a 17-inch sizzle crash.

What was most interesting about this whole process was what happened after the rehearsal. Paul came up to me and said he was blown away by the fact that I was doing everything that he requested. He was so encouraged and blessed by the way I was helping him find the right vibe for his music. He was stunned. Actually I didn't think it was that big of a deal. But I finally realized why he acted so surprised. Many times I have witnessed musicians giving an artist a hard time about his or her request to change something about the musician's approach to the job.

Please don't think I'm bragging. What I want you to realize is that serving people brings a blessing to a situation. Living in WWJD (What Would Jesus Do?) mode is so much better than going the other way. When I mess that up and choose not to live by that code, then everyone, myself included, is miserable. And I've blown it enough times to know that it's true. I hope you don't mind if I don't give you an example of those situations.

My Own Story

Well, okay! Just one personal story! No names though, to protect the innocent. I was playing drums at a conference, and we were recording the event. The producer had been asking for one change after another right up until the sound check before the recorded service. "Could you try this feel?" "Could you do this dynamic change in the first verse?" "Oh, and try a different tempo!" And blah, blah, blah. Snap!

Carl turns to the producer and says, "Look, I've played on hundreds of records. You should trust me that this is working fine. You're wearing the band out with all of your suggestions. Blah, blah, blah . . ."

The Holy Spirit starts speaking to my heart. "Carl, what are you doing?"

"Yes, Lord?"

"Carl, what are you doing? I thought you were here to serve. Did you forget what I made you for? What would I do?"

So this was the impression I was getting in my head even as I was talking back to the producer. I was basically getting a pretty good spiritual spanking in the middle of this exchange of words I was having, and it changed my heart.

So, Carl turns back to the producer and says, "Sorry, bro, whatever you want. I'll give you my best shot! This project is your vision and your responsibility, and I'm here to help you reach that goal."

I even went to him later and apologized for being out of line. That would be called "repentance." He said it was no big deal. I appreciated him being gracious, but made sure we were in a good place before we left the conversation. By the way, we're still friends, and we still work together. Recently we were working on another recording together, and he specifically recalled that event and our exchange. He never forgot how impressed he was that I was willing to set aside my own opinion to serve whatever he wanted to try for the sake of being creative and working with new ideas. Being willing to humble myself changed everything.

Humbling yourself and serving is not always easy. In fact, most of the time, it is a real challenge. After all of these years of music and ministry, the tests still come. I used to think that I would grow out of them. But what I've learned is that I've grown in the midst of them. And I bless you as fellow minstrels of the Lord as you continue to grow in the middle of all of your journeys in music and ministry. Thanks for having hearts that serve as you lay solid foundations of groove for all your bands.

Press on!

serve one another in love.

—Galatians 5:13

Appendix: About the DVD-ROM

Video Tutorials and Examples

The DVD-ROM included in this book contains examples of the more technical material found in *The Worship Drum Book*, including demonstrations of cymbal tone and matching, drum tuning, drum microphone placement, and mixing techniques. There are also excerpts from Carl's *Drum Grooves for Worship* DVD that relate specifically to chapter 11, along with some very helpful ideas about playing to a click track. These tutorials all support the concepts presented in the text.

1. Choosing Cymbals

See Carl's cymbal setup and hear his thoughts on selecting cymbals.

2. Miking Drums: The Big Picture

Carl briefly compares the way drums sound naturally to the way they sound when they're miked.

3. Testing Drumheads

This clip shows a great technique to use when selecting drumheads.

4. Kick Drum Tuning

Carl demonstrates a popular approach to tuning the bass drum and also offers some additional options.

5. Basic Snare Drum Tuning and Wire Adjustments

In this tutorial, we learn that in addition to proper tuning, wire tension makes an important difference in the sound of a snare drum.

6. Tom Tuning and Pitch Interval Choices

See how to find the resonant pitch of a drum, and hear the advantage in tuning the toms in your kit to more broadly spaced intervals.

7. Groove No. 1 from the "Drum Grooves for Worship" Chapter

The basic eighth-note feel is explained and demonstrated while playing to a metronome.

8. Groove No. 2 from the "Drum Grooves for Worship" Chapter

In this clip, Carl demonstrates the importance of getting the filler sixteenth-notes to feel just right. These grooves are very popular in all styles of modern music.

9. Groove No. 3 from the "Drum Grooves for Worship" Chapter

Using sixteenth-notes played in a single stroke roll technique gives this groove its nickname, "the train."

10. Groove No. 4 from the "Drum Grooves for Worship" Chapter

Learning to play slow ballads well is one of the trickiest things a drummer must do. This video demonstrates some fantastic exercises and techniques to keep your groove solid.

11. Groove No. 5 from the Drum Grooves for Worship Chapter

This classic 6/8 feel is used extensively in modern worship songs. Learn how to count and feel triplet-based grooves.

12. Groove No. 6 from the "Drum Grooves for Worship" Chapter

Understanding how to play shuffle and swing grooves is important for all drummers. Even though these grooves are rare in modern worship, this video emphasizes the need to be a drummer who is ready for anything.

13. Groove No. 7 from the "Drum Grooves for Worship" Chapter

See how to make odd time signatures feel natural. As with the other groove demonstrations, you'll see how the click track is also a necessary tool for developing a solid feel when playing grooves with odd time signatures.

Index

About the Author

Carl Albrecht has been a professional drummer and percussionist for over 30 years. He has a bachelor's degree in composition and arranging with an emphasis in percussion studies from Webster University in St. Louis, Missouri. Although Albrecht has performed in a variety of musical situations, he is mostly recognized in the modern praise and worship movement. He has played on over 80 Integrity Music projects, Maranatha Praise Band recordings 7 through 10, and numerous other Christian, pop, country, jazz, and commercial projects. Albrecht has worked with such artists as Paul Baloche, Don Moen, Ron Kenoly, Lenny LeBlanc, Bob Fitts, Paul Wilbur, Alvin Slaughter, Darrell Evans, Phil Driscoll, Koinonia, Abe Laboriel and Friends, Kim Hill, Paul Overstreet, LeAnn Rimes, Connie Smith, Don Potter, Jason Upton, Travis Cottrell, Dustin Smith, the smooth jazz group Quad Venti, producer Tom Brooks, and many others.

Carl Albrecht is one of the most honored and respected worship drummers in the world today. He has played on hundreds of recordings and tours, and his passionate musical ministry has drawn people around the globe into the presence of God. Besides being a supportive team player to many artists, he is equally known as an inspiring speaker and teacher at many seminars and worship events. In addition, his instructional DVD series has achieved an Editor's Choice Award on worshipmusic.com.

Carl Albrecht currently lives in Nashville, doing recording sessions, producing, and writing, as well as continuing to appear on various tours, conferences, and seminar events.

He officially endorses and uses Yamaha Drums, Vater drumsticks, Evans drumheads, SKB cases, Shure microphones, PreSonus preamps, and Cubase recording software. He also unofficially endorses Meinl cymbals and percussion instruments. You can visit his website at www. carlalbrecht.com.